THE

DEE BRESTIN

BIBLE STUDY SERIES

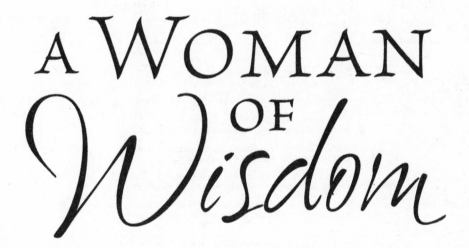

A WOMAN
OF
Wisdom

David C Cook

transforming lives together

The Dee Brestin Series

From David C. Cook

BOOKS

The Friendships of Women

The Friendships of Women Devotional Journal

We Are Sisters

We Are Sisters Devotional Journal

BIBLE STUDY GUIDES

A WOMAN OF LOVE
Using Our Gift for Intimacy (Ruth)

A WOMAN OF FAITH
Overcoming the World's Influences
(Esther)

A WOMAN OF CONFIDENCE
Triumphing over Life's Trials
(1 Peter)

A WOMAN OF PURPOSE
Walking with the Savior (Luke)

A WOMAN OF WORSHIP
Praying with Power (10 Psalms with a
music CD)

A WOMAN OF HOSPITALITY
Loving the Biblical Approach
(Topical)

A WOMAN OF MODERATION
Breaking the Chains of Poor Eating
Habits (Topical)

A WOMAN OF CONTENTMENT
Insight into Life's Sorrows
(Ecclesiastes)

A WOMAN OF BEAUTY
Becoming More Like Jesus
(1, 2, 3 John)

A WOMAN OF WISDOM
God's Practical Advice for Living
(Proverbs)

**A WOMAN OF HEALTHY RELA-
TIONSHIPS**
Sisters, Mothers, Daughters, Friends
(Topical)

**THE FRIENDSHIPS OF WOMEN
BIBLE STUDY GUIDE** correlates
with **THE FRIENDSHIPS OF
WOMEN**

A WOMAN OF WISDOM
Published by David C. Cook
4050 Lee Vance View
Colorado Springs, CO 80918 U.S.A.

David C. Cook Distribution Canada
55 Woodslee Avenue, Paris, Ontario, Canada N3L 3E5

David C. Cook U.K., Kingsway Communications
Eastbourne, East Sussex BN23 6NT, England

David C. Cook and the graphic circle C logo
are registered trademarks of Cook Communications Ministries.

ISBN 978-0-7814-4332-6

Interior Design: Nancy L. Haskins
Cover Design: Greg Jackson, Thinkpen Design, llc

Printed in the United States of America

First Edition 2006

2 3 4 5 6 7 8 9 10

Contents

To Jan Silvious,

for whose wisdom
and friendship I am forever thankful

Introduction

At the age of twenty-one, I was a foolish wife and mother who, as Proverbs 14:1 describes, was tearing down her home with her own hands. God in His mercy rescued me at that time in salvation, but I still was in desperate need of wisdom for how to turn my home around! Our toddler was in complete control of me, my marriage was suffering, and all the advice books I read on marriage and mothering conflicted with each other. And then! I discovered Proverbs. Here was the "Maker's Manual on Marriage and Mothering." Not only did the wisdom in this book turn my marriage around, but it certainly contributed, along with God's grace, to my five grown children walking with the Lord, to rich and deep friendships, and to having confidence for decisions in so many practical matters. Great Christians throughout the ages have spent time daily in Psalms (for their vertical relationship with God) and also in Proverbs (for their horizontal relationship with others.)

Along with studying Proverbs, we will look at scriptural women who model the characteristics we find in this book. Having real life examples will bring the proverbs to life, helping you become the woman of wisdom God longs for you to be.

It's helpful to know that proverbs are general truths, rather than promises. For example, generally speaking, the lazy man becomes poor, the child trained up in the way he should go becomes godly, and a gentle answer will turn away wrath. In each case, you may be able to find an exception, for proverbs are not promises, but general truths to guide you wisely through life.

It is vital to remember we do not have the power in ourselves to obey the proverbs. Continually cry out for the mercy of God for the power to obey. Begin your time each day by turning to the back of guide and singing a few of the praise choruses provided. Our horizontal relationships will never be right unless our relationship with God is right. So begin with God, praising Him, crying out for mercy, and asking Him to set your heart to obey His wisdom.

Memory verses are part of each lesson. A sheet with all the verses is at the back of this guide. Cut it out and place it on your mirror or refrigerator!

Leader's helps are also at the back of this guide.

Determine now to be faithful in doing your homework. For your convenience, each chapter is divided into five days, for your daily devotions. Also, determine to be faithful in your attendance to your small group. For, as you will see, though faithfulness is rare in our world, a woman of wisdom is faithful.

One

She Loves and Fears God
Sapphira/The Hebrew Midwives

eventeen-year-old Charity Allen was offered a role on "Another World," a successful NBC daytime drama. Stardom, a seven figure salary, and a limousine were dangled in front of her eyes. Her family's days of living in a trailer could be over! Though the producer assured her she wouldn't have to compromise her Christian convictions, the script revealed her character would, among other things, have an affair with a married man. Though the producer argued that these are "adolescent issues that all teens struggle with," Charity responded:

How many teens do you know who have affairs with married men?
I don't know any! And I'm not going to portray one, either.

Despite pressure from producers, and even from her teachers, Charity stood firm. Her foremost desire was to live a life that was pleasing to God and this didn't fit! "Another World" cast a different girl. Charity gave up being a star. Or did she? Susie Shellenberger, in writing about Charity for *Brio* (Focus on the Family's May, 1994 magazine for girls), said that Charity, in choosing to live a life that is pleasing to God, shines like a star amidst a "crooked and depraved generation" (Phil. 2:14–15).

WARMUP

Read over the Introduction together and then have each woman share her name, a little about herself, and what she hopes to gain from the group.

Read the following passage:

> *In the fear of the Lord one has strong confidence, and one's children will have a refuge. The fear of the Lord is a fountain of life, so that one may avoid the snares of death* (Prov. 14:26–27, NRSV).

Describe some "snares" you might be saved from by fearing God. Discuss this in terms of the example of Dee's life or Charity's life as well.

SCRIPTURE STUDY
The Scripture study is divided into five days, for five personal quiet times with the Lord.

DAY I
. . . .

A Woman of Wisdom Fears the Lord
The book of Proverbs begins and ends with stressing the importance of fearing the Lord.

> *The fear of the LORD is the beginning of knowledge, but fools despise wisdom and discipline* (Prov. 1:7).

> *Charm is deceptive, and beauty is fleeting; but a woman who fears the LORD is to be praised* (Prov. 31:30).

Memorize Proverbs 31:30 by taking a word at a time. (Charm; Charm is; Charm is deceptive ...) A list of memory verses can be found at the end of this guide. Tear them out and hang them on your mirror or above your kitchen sink!

1. Read through Proverbs 1.

A. What reasons can you find in Proverbs 1:1–6 for studying proverbs?

To know wisdom, instruction, give discernment receive instruction in behavior, righteousness

B. What foundational principle is given in Proverbs 1:7? What contrast is given? *The Fear of the Lord is the beginning of wisdom Fools despise wisdom and instruction*

C. What basic warning does the father give the son, and why, in Proverbs 1:8–19?

Do not walk in the way of fools Keep your feet from their path It will take away your life

8

D. Who is crying out in Proverbs 1:20–33? What reasons are given for listening to her? *Wisdom, she will pour out her spirit on you I will make my words known to you. You will live securely and be at ease from the dread of evil*

Two voices, personified as women, cry out to us throughout Proverbs: the "woman wisdom" and the "woman folly." The voice of wisdom is the Lord, the source of all wisdom; and the woman folly has her origin in the evil one, the father of lies. The woman folly appears in various forms throughout Scripture—for example, she is often the "harlot Babylon" who is always seducing, always lying, and often succeeding in bring ruin to men.

2. Why do you think the fear of the Lord is the beginning of wisdom? Was that true in your life? If so, explain how. *If you fear God you will not trust in yourself but will put your trust in God and His words.*

Throughout the Old and New Testaments, we are exhorted to fear God. This includes the concept of reverence, but also an awakening to the realization of God's holiness and wrath at unrighteousness. This fear helps us understand our need for a Savior. Jesus makes this clear when He says:

Do not be afraid of those who kill the body but cannot kill the soul. Rather, be afraid of the One who can destroy both soul and body in hell (Matt. 10:28).

In my life, it was the fear of hell that drew me, at first, to Him. When I surrendered to Him, trusting in His payment for my sin on the cross, God delivered me from my fear of hell. Now my love for God is stronger than my fear of Him, but I still fear Him, in the way a child who respects her father fears disobeying and displeasing Him. *I am glad* I fear God, for that fear has saved me from many a snare!

3. The "fool" in Proverbs is someone who does not fear God. Why is it foolish not to fear God? *He is the one we will give an account to one day. He is the one who gives eternal life.*

If we would know God, it is vital that we face the truth concerning His wrath, however unfashionable it may be, and however strong our initial prejudices against it. Otherwise, we shall not understand the gospel of salvation from wrath, nor the propitiatory achievement of the cross, nor the wonder of the redeeming love of God. (J. I. Packer, *Knowing God*, InterVarsity, p. 152.)

DAY 2

Fear God, and Fear Nothing Else

When I look back over my life, I can see so many snares from which the fear of the Lord delivered me. So often sin seems like the easy way out, but instead, it leads to great pain and regrets. My first pregnancy was unexpected and untimely—and pressure was put on me from my husband's family to abort. But though I was not yet in a personal relationship with Christ, I did fear God enough to know I couldn't take a life. Oh my—how I would have regretted that! Likewise, as a young and foolish bride, I played with the idea of divorce, but again, I had a growing fear of the Lord, so I turned from that. Within a year, God turned our marriage around and gave us 38 amazing years—a marriage that became absolutely precious. How foolish I was! I almost destroyed the most precious gifts in my life—but my awareness of God's holiness protected them.

The fear of the Lord doesn't preserve you from all trouble, but from many snares. When trouble comes, and Jesus says it will, He will be with you. This year my precious husband Steve died of colon cancer at the age of 59. Though my grief is enormous, the Lord has been there for me, as husband, protector, provider, comforter. I absolutely know that I will see Steve again, for Christ has also conquered our last enemy: death. God *does* take care of those who fear Him. "As a father has compassion for his children, so the Lord has compassion on those who fear him" (Ps. 103:13, NRSV).

4. Read Proverbs 2.
   A. What are the ways a person can discern the fear and knowledge of God? (Prov. 2:1–5)

   B. What are some of the blessings of wisdom according to Proverbs 2:6–11?

   C. Describe the person wisdom will save you from according to Proverbs 2:12–15.

   D. Describe the person wisdom will save you from according to Proverbs 2:16–19.

   E. Look again at the adulteress in the above passage. What did she ignore according to verse 17? Why, do you think?

F. What contrast do you find in Proverbs 2:20–22? What do you think this means?

5. The woman folly will tell you that the happiest life is one in which you are free of God's rules. Sleep with whoever you want, watch whatever you please, eat as much as you like—and you will be happy. Yet those choices end, not in freedom, but in bondage. Meditate on Proverbs 2:11 and give some examples of how this has been or could be true in your life.

6. Martin Luther said, "Fear God and do as you please." Many have painted the fear of God as a negative, when it truly is a positive. What blessing from Proverbs 2 for fearing the Lord stands out to you and why?

7. What fears has the Lord delivered you from? Explain.

DAY 3

Sapphira, A Woman Who Trifled with God

The fear of the LORD adds length to life, but the years of the wicked are cut short (Prov. 10:27).

When I am inclined to embellish the truth to receive praise from others, may I remember Ananias and Sapphira! While there's nothing to indicate that this couple lost their salvation, they certainly lost years on earth and their reputations. Though God usually spares us His wrath, He is still sovereign, and may choose to discipline. It does seem that often believers in leadership who trifle with God are caught and humbled publicly.

Read Acts 4:32–37 as background.

8. Joseph was greatly loved by the body of believers, as evidenced by his nickname. What was it? What act of encouragement is recorded about him in this passage?

Read Acts 5:1–11.
9. Describe the incident in this passage and the effect it had on the church.

In this grace age, we are turning out mediocre saints who feel that since they are in Christ, they can live as they please. But I don't know of anything that will check sin quicker than a deep reverence for God. (Charles Swindoll, "Insight for Living," April 7, 1994.)

10. How did Peter give Sapphira a second chance to tell the truth? What do you think motivated her to lie?

11. Are you ever motivated to enhance your own significance? If possible, give an example. With whose significance should we be concerned?

Describe some ways that you can see a longing in your heart to bring glory to God.

12. Some Christians insist that if your husband asks you to do something immoral, you should submit because God will hold your husband—not you—accountable. How does this passage teach otherwise? Does this mean we should not submit to our husbands? Explain.

Review your memory work.

DAY 4

The Hebrew Midwives Feared God and Were Blessed

Lori, an unmarried college freshman, discovered she was pregnant. "Because I didn't want to face my parents, I had fleeting thoughts of abortion and even suicide, but my fear of God kept me from either. Today my parents and I cherish my three-year-old daughter and are so thankful God put His fear in me."

13. Read Proverbs 3.

A. List the blessings you can find in Proverbs 3:1–8 that come from listening, trusting, and fearing the Lord.

B. What specific warning and blessing is in Proverbs 3:9–10? Does your checkbook indicate that you truly love and honor God?

C. Why, according to verses 11–12, shouldn't we resent the Lord's rebuke?

D. In Proverbs 3:15, we are told "nothing you desire can compare with her" (wisdom). What do you desire? If you listed other things than godly wisdom, why might they not be as valuable?

E. What blessing will the person who preserves "sound judgment and discernment" experience according to Proverbs 3:21–26?

F. What warning is given in Proverbs 3:28? Why do you think we often hold back when we have a chance to speak kindly or to help someone?

14. Read Exodus 1:8–22.
   A. Describe the three plans Pharaoh had for reducing the number of the Israelites.

   B. How did the midwives foil plan B?

   C. Why did they refuse to cooperate? How did God respond?

   D. How does their story illustrate Proverbs 3:25–26?

   During World War II, Corrie ten Boom showed similar courage when she learned that a Jewish orphanage in Amsterdam was to be raided and the babies slaughtered. Dressed in the uniforms of Nazi soldiers who'd defected, thirty teenage boys drove up to the orphanage in trucks and demanded the babies. They took them from the arms of weeping workers who did not realize the babies were actually being saved. Years later Corrie had the privilege of meeting some of these children. In emotional greeting scenes, she hugged them and gave thanks to the Lord. (Joan Winmill Brown, *Corrie: The Lives She's Touched*, Revell, p. 31.)

15. Compare Proverbs 3:32b with Psalm 25:14. What amazing blessing is given to those who fear the Lord and do right? (*a* designates the first part of a verse, *b* designates the second part.)

Next week we will look at Mary of Bethany, who, alone among Jesus' followers, seemed to understand what He was saying about going to Jerusalem to die. He blessed her, helping her understand this mystery. What an example she is, therefore, of Proverbs 3:32b.

DAY 5

God Uses the Woman Who Fears Him

My sister Sally led me to the Lord when I was a young wife and mother. Because Sally knows "what it is to fear the Lord," she tried to persuade me to put my trust in Christ (2 Cor. 5:11). The Holy Spirit worked through my sister, and I was persuaded. When I told Sally that my opening chapter was on fearing the Lord and I was a bit apprehensive of a negative reaction, Sally firmly said: "There's no command in the Scripture with more blessings attached to it. Don't fear what others will think, Dee, fear God." Proverbs 29:25 warns: "Fear of man will prove to be a snare." I have come to see that the woman who loves and fears God is used mightily by Him, and the woman who fears others is paralyzed and fails to bear fruit.

In Proverbs 4 you can sense the emotion of a parent who loves his child dearly, and longs for him to truly hear and embrace what he is saying.

16. Read Proverbs 4.
   A. How early did this father impress on his son the importance of God's wisdom? Support your answer with a reference.

   B. Find five similar commands in Proverbs 4:14–15.

14

C. Is there a path God is longing for you to avoid? If so, what is it? Why, according to what you've learned so far, would it bless you to avoid it?

D. What admonition is given in verse 23 and why?

E. What are some specific ways you could apply verse 23?

17. In your life, think about how the fear of the Lord has led to fruitfulness. Can you share one with the group?

18. What do you think you will remember from this lesson? How will you apply it?

PRAYER TIME

Many people are intimidated by the idea of praying out loud. This guide will be gentle, leading you into this gradually. And no one will ever be forced to pray out loud.

Today, have each woman share a personal request. For example, she might ask, "I would like to grow closer to God" or "I need wisdom as a mother." Write these down, and pray for each other at home. Pay particular attention to the woman on your right, for whom you will pray daily.

Teach your group to sing "Father, I Adore You" (p. 114). (See the hints for leading music on the same page.)

Prayers & Praises

_____

_____

_____

_____

_____

_____

_____

_____

_____

_____

_____

_____

_____

Two

Her Heart Is Fully Devoted to Christ
Mary/Martha

Mary of Bethany is remembered for her devotion to Christ. She is the one who sat at his feet, and, as *The Message* paraphrases it, was "hanging on every word he said." She is the one that broke her alabaster jar at the feet of Jesus. Jesus canonized her on the spot for her devotion, saying, "Wherever this gospel is preached throughout the world, what she has done will also be told, in memory of her." Her fragrance, poured out on Him just days before His crucifixion, clung to Him, reminding Him, through the beatings, the crown of thorns, and the crucifixion, that there was one who loved Him, who was fully devoted to Him.

When we are devoted to Christ, when we cling to His teachings as "the apple of our eye," we are protected from the path that will lead to destruction. For example, it can be a deterrent to say: "Don't have an affair because God will be angry." However, even more effective is to be so in love with Jesus, so devoted to Him, that He fills the need that an affair can never fill. Devotion to Christ is its own protection from sin.

Proverbs 5—6 is a section filled with warnings to the young man about the adulterous woman. Yet he ignores these warnings, failing to keep them as "the apple of his eye," and we see him walk straight toward destruction in Proverbs 7.

The adulteress in Proverbs is often, literally, adulterous. However, we can apply her call to whatever siren voice calls us away from our devotion to

Christ and into the chains of sin. It may be the lure of laziness, over-eating, materialism, or an obsession with the praise of man.

The secret to not walking toward her house, to shutting our ears to her siren song, is keeping our heart fully devoted to Christ, to above all else, guard our heart.

WARMUP

Name one "siren voice" that calls you away from single-hearted devotion to Christ. (Give women the freedom to pass.)

SCRIPTURE STUDY
DAY I

• •

She Keeps Her Heart with All Diligence

The heart is key to all of life. Seventy-five times in the book of Proverbs alone (KJV) the word *heart* is used. The root reason for a ho-hum Christian life is a divided and distracted heart: a failure to keep our hearts with all diligence. Memorize the following:

> *Keep thy heart with all diligence; for out of it are the issues of life*
> (Prov. 4:23 KJV).

1. Put the above proverb in your own words.

Read Proverbs 5.
2. What reason does the father give the son in Proverbs 5:3–5 to stay away from the adulteress?

3. Now, identify the adulteress in your life. How might the warnings of Proverbs 5:3–5 be relevant to you?

4. What other reasons does the father give for "staying away?" In each, see if there might be a warning for you and your siren voice, whoever she is.
   A. Proverbs 5:8–9

B. Proverbs 5:11–14

5. Proverbs 5:15–20 shifts primarily to the positive, for reasons for his son to be true to his wife. What reasons are given?

As a young wife I made a plate for Steve that said: "Rejoice in the wife of your youth." Steve good-naturedly carried it to church potlucks and endured the smiles of others. Steve obeyed that passage—never even flirting, in our 39 years of marriage, with a beautiful nurse or patient. Our marriage was blessed, and I am so thankful that we never experienced the pain of unfaithfulness.

6. What additional reasons for avoiding the siren's voice are given in Proverbs 5:21–23?

7. The following passages in Proverbs give insight on how to keep our hearts with all diligence. Write down any principles you find in the passages for keeping your heart.

A. Proverbs 2:1–6

B. Proverbs 3:3–8

For Personal Reflection Only

8. Consider the following ways to keep your heart healthy. How could you improve in each?

A. Your daily time of Bible study and prayer:

B. Keeping the path clear between you and the Lord through confessing and turning from any sin:

C. Listening to Christian music or radio; reading Christian books or magazines:

Action Assignment

Plan when and where you will have your daily time of Bible study and prayer this week. Keep this appointment as diligently as you would keep appointments with people.

When will you meet with God?

Where will you meet with Him?

DAY 2

Her Devoted Heart
Protects Her from Snares

Review your memory work of Proverbs 4:23.

9. Read Proverbs 6.
   A. What snare is described in Proverbs 6:1–5?

If you feel led to help someone financially, give them the money. Loaning money or guaranteeing a loan is not wise. It leads to division, discord, and disaster.

   B. What snare is described in Proverbs 6:6–11? Have you been lazy about your time with God? What has worked for you to combat laziness in this area?

I have downloaded R. C. Sproul's sermons on my iPod and listen while I bike each morning. I have also learned if I don't spend time with the Lord first thing, I don't do it.

   C. What snare is described in Proverbs 6:12–15?

   D. In Proverbs 6:16–19 you find a list of things the Lord hates. "Six, no seven" is a poetic device showing this list is not exhaustive. A parallel can be made to the Beatitudes in that they list the contrasting positive attribute. For example, the Lord hates a haughty look, but blesses "the poor in spirit." He hates "hands that shed innocent blood," but sees "peace-makers as children of God." List each of the things the Lord hates and see if you can also list its opposite.

E. Proverbs 6:20–35 gives us more warnings against adultery. List three that stand out to you.

Review your memory passage.

DAY 3

She Guards His Teachings as the Apple of Her Eye

We now hear a story of a foolish boy who ignored the teachings of his father. He takes a walk one evening toward the home of an adulteress. If we do not guard our Father's teachings as the apple of our eye, we can be just as foolish, walking toward temptation, making provision for the flesh, and sliding toward destruction.

10. Read Proverbs 7.
  A. What three pictures are given in Proverbs verses 2–4?

  B. What is being stressed by the above?

  C. What crucial mistake did the young man make in Proverbs 7:6–9?

  D. How did this show that he was not keeping the teachings as the apple of his eye?

  E. In what ways do you tend to be "walking along in the direction of her house"?

F. Who came out to meet him, and what were her persuasive arguments? (Prov. 7:10–20)

"I have fellowship offerings at home" simply meant she had fresh meat left-over from the temple sacrifice. Her religion meant no more to her spiritually than does the celebration of Christmas to many today.

G. Describe his destruction at the close of the chapter, drawing upon the word pictures.

H. Is there an application for you?

DAY 4

A Devoted Heart: Mary of Bethany

A Distracted Heart: Martha of Bethany

Review your memory work of Proverbs 4:23.

We are told that Jesus loved both Mary and Martha of Bethany (John 11:5), and many times the one who had "no place to lay his head" found rest and refreshment in their hospitable home. The scene we remember the best, however, is when Jesus gently rebuked Martha. He protected Mary from her sister's rebuke, telling Martha that it was actually Martha who was out of His will. She was worried about so many things, but only one thing was truly necessary. Mary had found it, and it would not be taken from her.

What is the most important thing?

Read Luke 10:38–42

11. As this tends to be a familiar passage, look at it carefully. Write down any phrases which describe Mary. Write down any phrases which describe Martha.

Mary:

Martha:

12. What did Jesus tell Martha?

13. What is "the better part," or "the most important thing" according to the following passages?

    A. Deuteronomy 6:5

    B. Matthew 22:36–37

    C. Revelation 2:2–5

The church at Ephesus was working hard, not tolerating evil—yet they had missed the most important thing: loving Jesus. This church did not respond to the rebuke of Jesus, for the church died—the lampstand was removed.

14. What was Jesus telling Martha?

DAY 5

Martha of Bethany, a Teachable Heart

Mary of Bethany, an Enlightened Heart

Often we only remember Martha as the critical sister in the kitchen. But there is much more to Martha. She had a teachable heart, responding to the discipline of the Lord, as Proverbs urges us to do again and again. Karen Mains writes:

> *Spiritual awakening always begins with cleansing. It begins in the heart of an individual who suddenly says to himself, "I'm dirty." And that is painful, particularly if we've been pretending all along to be clean. We go kicking and protesting to the water basin—we'll give our faces a swipe, but we don't want to wash behind our ears. . . . But pure joy can be experienced in the bathtub . . . God delights in the spiritual bathing of his earthly children and he wraps them, cleansed, in the wooly towel of his love and approval* (Karen Mains, *With My Whole Heart*, Multnomah, p. 19).

The next time we see Mary and Martha is in John 11, when their brother Lazarus becomes ill. Martha is the confrontive sister: strong, bold, and outspoken. Yet her heart is now a listening heart, wanting to hear and understand what Jesus has to say to her.

15. Read John 11:1–27

  A. What did the sisters do when Lazarus became ill (John 11:3)?

  B. What did Jesus do (John 11:6)?

  C. When did Jesus finally arrive (John 11:17)?

  D. What does Martha do (John 11:20–22)?

  E. What challenging question does Jesus ask Martha (John 11:26)?

  F. Jesus was asking if Martha believed He was the Christ. Why might that have been a painful and difficult question to answer affirmatively in light of what had just happened?

  G. How does Martha respond (John 11:27)? What does this tell you about Martha?

It is obvious that even now Martha is not expecting Jesus to raise Lazarus from the dead. She believes there will one day be a resurrection, but she certainly isn't anticipating what is about to happen. When Jesus asks the men to roll away the stone, again, she confronts Jesus. Again, she responds to His gentle rebuke. And, again, she is blessed.

16. Read John 11:38–44

  A. Why didn't Martha want the men to remove the stone?

  B. How does Jesus gently rebuke her?

  C. She must have given a nod of her head, for the men roll away the stone. What amazing blessing awaited her? How do you think she felt?

17. God may rebuke us through His Word, His Spirit, or through one of His servants. Read the following and explain why we should listen carefully to rebuke. What do you learn from the following proverbs about having a teachable heart?

    A. Proverbs 1:22–33

    B. Proverbs 12:1

    C. Proverbs 13:18

    D. Proverbs 15:31–32

18. Do you have a teachable heart like Martha did? Can you think of a time recently when you listened to rebuke from God or a friend and changed something? If so, share.

    Dawson Trotman, who founded the International Discipleship Ministry of Navigators, said that whenever he is criticized, he always takes it into his prayer closet with the Lord and asks God to show him if there is a kernel of truth in the criticism (Dawson Trotman, *Daws*, NavPress).

19. Read John 12:1–11
    A. Describe Mary of Bethany's courageous act.

    B. What does Jesus tell Judas when Judas objects?

Matthew 26:12–13 records a fuller response from Jesus: "When she poured this perfume on my body, she did it to prepare me for burial. I tell you the truth, wherever this gospel is preached throughout the world, what she has done will also be told, in memory of her." God rewarded Mary's whole-hearted devotion with a rare enlightenment. In his study Bible, C. I. Scofield comments:

> "Mary of Bethany, alone of our Lord's followers, comprehended His thrice-repeated announcement of His coming death and resurrection."

God enlightens those who hunger and thirst for Him.

20. How can a devoted heart to Jesus protect you from temptation? Be specific and personal.

PRAYER TIME

An unintimidating form of group prayer is "conversational prayer," also called "popcorn prayer." Each person lifts up a personal request, perhaps based on the last question in this lesson. Then a few others support her with sentences. Then, when the "popping" stops, another woman lifts up her request. Close by singing "Father, I Adore You" (p. 114). This song can also be sung in a round.

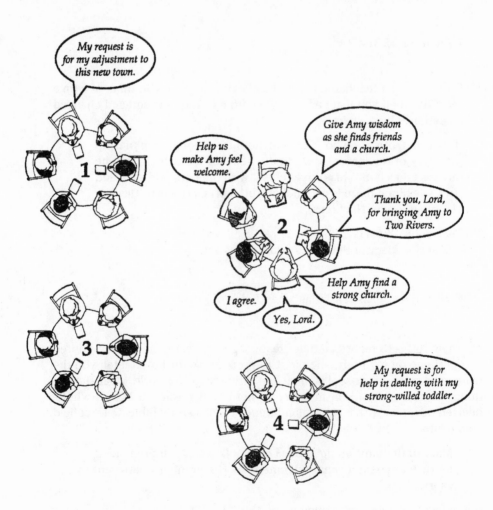

Three

She Speaks with Wisdom
Penninah/Hannah

Yesterday I became very angry with Beth, our thirteen-year-old daughter whom we adopted a year ago from an orphanage in Bangkok. Ostensibly I was angry because Beth hadn't finished the laundry. After losing my temper with her, I went into another room to cool down. Sensing a check from the Holy Spirit, I defended myself. *But, Lord, it was right for me to scold her. She told me she'd finished the laundry and she hadn't.*

The Lord revealed to me that while speaking the truth in love was appropriate, losing my temper was not. The real reason for my disproportionate anger was that I was feeling hurt that Beth isn't warmer and more loving to me. The root problem was not the unfinished laundry, and not even disobedience, but my lack of forgiveness toward Beth, my lack of understanding toward a child who has built a wall around herself. I'd been storing up hurt in my heart, keeping a record of slights, and eventually unleashed that hurt over a load of unfolded socks.

Jesus says: "The good man brings good things out of the good stored up in his heart, and the evil man brings evil things out of the evil stored up in his heart. For out of the overflow of his heart his mouth speaks" (Luke 6:45). A woman of wisdom speaks with kindness and wisdom, because that is what is stored up in her heart.

WARMUP

Go around, giving women the freedom to pass, and ask: Think about a significant conversation that you had with someone recently that was to you "a fountain of life" (Prov. 10:11). What about it made it refreshing?

On-the-Spot Action Assignment

In every discussion group, there are usually women who are too quick to speak up and others who are too slow to speak up. This exercise is to help you discern whether you lean toward either being a monopolizer or a wallflower. Your leader will give each woman five pennies. Every time you speak, put a penny in your lap. After you've spent your pennies, let the others speak. And everyone should spend at least two of their pennies!

SCRIPTURE STUDY
DAY 1

She Understands How Her Heart Affects Her Speech

Review your first two memory passages:
> *Charm is deceptive, and beauty is fleeting; but a woman who fears the Lord is to be praised* (Prov. 31:30).

> *Keep thy heart with all diligence; for out of it are the issues of life* (Prov. 4:23, KJV).

Now add the following:
> *She speaks with wisdom, and faithful instruction is on her tongue* (Prov. 31:26).

1. Explain how the above passages are related.

> When I am depleted spiritually, I become angry more quickly and either start a quarrel or enter one at the first provocation. When my walk with God is vital, somehow He keeps my emotional well-being stable. A time of drinking deeply from the river of His delights brings me joy and peace (Carole Mayhall, *Words That Hurt, Words That Heal*, NavPress, pp. 65–66).

2. In each of the following, explain the heart's effect on the tongue.

   A. *Out of the same mouth come praise and cursing. My brothers, this should not be. Can both fresh water and salt water flow from the same spring? My brothers, can a fig tree bear olives, or a grapevine bear figs? Neither can a salt spring produce fresh water* (James 3:10–12).

   B. *The heart of the righteous weighs its answers; but the mouth of the wicked gushes evil* (Prov. 15:28).

   C. *A wise man's heart guides his mouth, and his lips promote instruction* (Prov. 16:23).

3. What ideas do you have for guiding mealtime conversations with friends or family so that they become a "fountain of life"?

My husband made a family policy not to use mealtimes to discuss problems, discipline, or schedules, but instead to reserve that time for bonding and encouragement. Often we ask a question (What was your high and low point today?), discuss an ethical dilemma (*Ungame* or *Scruples* game cards are great for this!), or read a Scripture passage and share reflections on it.

4. Jesus says that out of the overflow of the heart the mouth speaks (Matt. 12:34b). If the heart is full of football, that's going to be the topic of conversation! What are your most frequent topics of conversation?

If the above list deals primarily with transitory things, what life changes could you make so that the overflow of your heart would spill forth eternally encouraging things?

In Proverbs 8, wisdom is again personified as a person. Many have equated this person with Jesus, and surely, it is true that there are many parallels, and in Christ are all the treasures of wisdom and knowledge. (Col.1:15–20; 2:3) But because wisdom appears to be a creation of God, it is unlikely that wisdom here is identical to Jesus Christ. (Allen Ross, *The Expositor's Bible Commentary,* Vol 5, p. 943.)

5. Read Proverbs 8.

A. To whom does wisdom call and why? (Prov. 8:1–5)

B. Describe the wisdom of God according to verses 6–8.

C. Who has been blessed and how by wisdom? (Prov. 8:11–21)

D. When did God create wisdom and how was it "the craftsman at his side?" (Prov. 8:22–31)

E. What contrasting choices and results are given in verses 32–37?

Action Assignment

6. "The mouth of the righteous is a fountain of life" (Prov. 10:11). Choose to do one of the following this week.

A. Read a Christian book this week and journal one new thought to share with the group.

B. Listen to Christian radio and journal one new thought to share with the group. (If you're not keeping a journal, start! Record what you learn from God's Word, sermons, books, etc. This exercise alone will change your heart and its overflow!)

C. Download sermons on your iPod by going to oneplace.com. I particularly recommend John Piper, Kay Arthur, and Beth Moore. My favorite is R. C. Sproul—find him on ligonier.com. Another great resource is preachingtodayaudio.com Report on what you downloaded.

DAY 2

She Refrains from Boasting and Quarreling

Part of "training up our children" is to teach them these proverbs, to help them put a reign on their tongues. One summer our daughter Sally worked in a secular sports camp for boys. They often boasted, quarreled, or picked on the smaller boys. The proverbs were helpful to her in setting and reinforcing boundaries. She also, on the advice of a mentor who raised godly sons, had them say 10 nice things to someone if she heard them say one unkind thing to that person.

At the root of evil speech is a prideful and uncharitable heart, which we all, by nature, have. The antidote is spending time in the presence of Jesus, for then we see ourselves as we ought, are filled with His love, and find ourselves overcoming our tendency to boast, gossip, lie, or lose our temper. We will fail, so we must continually be living in repentance and crying out for mercy for the power to obey.

7. Record the main point of the following proverbs in your own words.

A. *Let another praise you, and not your own mouth; someone else, and not your own lips* (Prov. 27:2).

If you want people to think well of you, do not speak well of yourself (Pascal)..

B. *It is not good to eat too much honey, nor is it honorable to seek one's own honor* (Prov. 25:27).

Read the following passages for insight on quarrelling.

But the wisdom that comes from heaven is first of all pure; then peace-loving, considerate, submissive, full of mercy and good fruit, impartial and sincere. Peacemakers who sow in peace raise a harvest of righteousness. What causes fights and quarrels among you? Don't they come from your desires that battle within you? You want something but don't get it. You kill and covet, but you cannot have what you want. You quarrel and fight (James 3:17—4:2a).

Only by pride cometh contention: but with the well advised is wisdom (Prov. 13:10, KJV).

8. What is the source of quarrels, according to the above?

How can you discern between a healthy difference of opinion and a quarrel?

9. Anger is not necessarily sinful, for Jesus became angry. However, how we handle anger *can* be sinful. Read the following passages and summarize what you learn about dealing with or expressing anger.

31

A. *And the Lord's servant must not quarrel; instead, he must be kind to everyone, able to teach, not resentful* (2 Tim. 2:24).

B. *It is honorable to refrain from strife, but every fool is quick to quarrel* (Prov. 20:3 NRSV).

C. *Do not let the sun go down while you are still angry, and do not give the devil a foothold* (Eph. 4:26b–27).

What divides and severs true Christian groups and Christians— what leaves a bitterness that can last for 20, 30, or 40 years is not the issue of doctrine or belief which caused the differences in the first place. Invariably it is lack of love—and the bitter things that are said by true Christians in the midst of differences. These stick in the mind like glue. . . . It is these things— these unloving attitudes and words—that cause the stench that the world can smell. . . . But Jesus did give the mark that will arrest the attention of the world. . . . What is it? The love that true Christians show for each other and not just for their own party (Francis Schaeffer, "The Mark of a Christian" in *The Church at the End of the 20th Century,* InterVarsity, p. 144).

DAY 3

She Is Quick to Listen, Slow to Speak, and Slow to Become Angry

With company coming for dinner, Carole grimly tackled the dirty job of cleaning the barbecue grill. Her husband, Jack, was resting with his feet up on the ottoman, having just come in from his new exercise program. When Carole came in for more paper towels, he told her proudly, "I walked five miles today."

Without a thought, Carole said: "Boy, just think of all you could have accomplished with that kind of energy." Seeing the joy of accomplishment drain from her husband's face, Carole felt convicted. She said, "I wanted to reach out and pull the words back.

... I apologized profusely and Jack said he forgave me. But the words had been said. I could not undo that. I remembered the verse that says, 'He who guards his lips guards his soul, but he who speaks rashly will come to ruin' (Prov. 13:3)" (Carole Mayhall, *Words that Hurt, Words that Heal,* NavPress, pp. 45–46).

10. Read the following proverbs and then describe the various kinds of damage a reckless woman might cause or a thoughtful woman might avoid.

   A. *An evil man is trapped by his sinful talk, but a righteous man escapes trouble* (Prov. 12:13).

   B. *Reckless words pierce like a sword* (Prov. 12:18a).

   C. *A harsh word stirs up anger* (Prov. 15:1b).

   D. *When words are many, sin is not absent, but he who holds his tongue is wise* (Prov. 10:19).

11. Give an example of trouble you caused or avoided by how you used or controlled your tongue.

12. Read Proverbs 9.
   A. How is a person's character revealed by rebuke according to Proverbs 9:7–9?

   B. How well do you receive criticism? Explain.

   C. Two women are calling in this chapter (1–6 and 13–18) What contrasting results will occur for those who turn in to each?

DAY 4

She Consciously Uses Her Tongue for Good

How thankful I am for godly friends who affirm me, who draw out the deep waters of my soul with questions, and who sharpen me with discussions out of the overflow of their own rich hearts! They understand "the tongue has the power of life and death" (Prov. 18:21) and use it to bring life.

Whereas Proverbs 1—9 seem to be orderly, Proverbs 10—22:16 defy any orderly plan, but are simply a collection of proverbs. We will continue, however, to read through proverbs, giving you the opportunity to highlight any that are particularly speaking to you at this time in your life.

13. Read Proverbs 10. What proverb or proverbs particularly stood out to you at this time in your life and why?

14. In Proverbs 10, find at least three descriptions of a fool. (Not a foolish person, but a fool. Fools are hardened and there is much less hope for them than for a foolish person.)

15. Read the following passages carefully. Then list some ways the tongue can be used for good.

   A. *An anxious heart weighs a man down, but a kind word cheers him up* (Prov. 12:25).

   B. *Pleasant words are a honeycomb, sweet to the soul and healing to the bones* (Prov. 16:24).

   C. *Perfume and incense bring joy to the heart, and the pleasantness of one's friend springs from his earnest counsel* (Prov. 27:9).

On-the-Spot Action Assignment

If time permits, go around the room and have each woman say one affirming sentence about the woman on her right. (You could divide into groups of three or four to do this more quickly.)

16. Thoughtful, affirming, pleasant, and wise words bless others, but they also impact the giver. Explain the following verse.

   A. *From the fruit of his lips a man is filled with good things as surely as the work of his hands rewards him* (Prov. 12:14).

   B. How have you been rewarded by using your tongue for good?

   C. How could you better put Proverbs 12:14 into practice with others?

17. To what does Proverbs 20:5 compare the heart of man? What can a friend of understanding do?

Have you ever had the experience of not understanding your own heart, or hurt, or reasons for doing something—but a friend was able to draw you out and help you to understand yourself? If you can remember a specific instance, share.

In your personal quiet time, use your tongue for good by singing praises to God, using the songs in the back of this guide.

DAY 5

Penninah and Hannah

Penninah and Hannah were both married to the same man. In addition to the pain of this relationship, each woman had her own private pain. Penninah responded to that pain foolishly, and Hannah responded wisely.

Read 1 Samuel 1:1–11. (In discussion, read only verses 6–11.)

18. Describe Penninah's private pain. How did she respond to it?

What kind of feelings tempt someone to behave as Penninah did?

19. Describe Hannah's private pain. How did she respond to it?

When our cup is jostled, what spills out reveals what is inside. How would you describe Hannah's heart, and how do you think it got that way?

Read 1 Samuel 1:12–28. (In discussion, read verses 12–16.)

20. How did Hannah respond to Eli?

How did God bless Hannah? Do you think the story might have turned out differently had Hannah become angry with Eli?

Hannah kept her vow to God and relinquished Samuel. How do you think she was able to do it?

21. Read Hannah's song in 1 Samuel 2:1–10 and list everything you can discover which Hannah knew about God.

Hannah's song of praise may very well have been the inspiration for Mary's Magnificat. Hannah and Mary both regarded themselves as "handmaidens" of the Lord and were eager to serve their great God. Most of us pray in hard times, but a truly godly woman also prays in good times.

22. Does this song give you any insight as to why Hannah was able to be quiet when Penninah taunted her?

What helps you control your tongue when someone is unkind to you?

23. Which response to pain was more effective: Penninah's or Hannah's? Why?

24. What do you learn from this story to apply to your own life?

For Personal Reflection Only

How many of your pennies did you spend? Do you talk too much, too easily, or too long? Do you talk too little and deprive the group of rich interaction? How could you do better?

One of the most difficult problems for any Bible study discussion facilitator is the monopolizer. If you know you have a tendency toward monopolizing, ask a friend to sit next to you and give you a gentle pat when you need it. A group is also impoverished if the shy people never share. Mark the questions where you feel you might have something to offer, and then speak up!

PRAYER TIME

Spend some time using your tongues in praise to God, encouraging the women to say simple sentences of thanks or praise. Then close by singing the "Doxology" (p. 101).

Prayers & Praises

_____

_____

_____

_____

_____

_____

_____

_____

_____

_____

_____

_____

_____

_____

_____

Four

She Is Discreet
The Haughty Women of Zion/
The Holy Women of Old

The next two lessons consider similar attributes: discretion and prudence. They are almost interchangeable, as both words communicate careful choices on the basis of wisdom. The slight difference, perhaps, is that we often associate discretion with the impression one makes on others. The word *discreet* can also mean "set apart." There are, for example, "discreet notes" in music, where you can tell one from another. A woman who is discreet will be different from the women who listen to the wisdom of the world.

It is also possible to be discreet without knowing the Lord. Often women from a strong social upbringing are skilled in manners and dress. Two women that come to mind are Princess Diana and Jacqueline Kennedy Onassis. When Jacqueline Kennedy died, the following tributes were typical:

> *She was a connection to a time that was more dignified, more private, an America in which standards were higher and clearer and elegance meant something. . . . She had manners, the kind that remind us that manners spring from a certain moral view—that you do tribute to the world and the people in it by being kind and showing respect, by sending the note and the flowers, by being loyal, and cheering a friend (Peggy Noonan, Time Magazine, 5/30/94).*

> *I am struck most by how we reflect on her taste and passion for the highest of excellence, while we live in a base society. We mourn the*

> *loss of her desire for privacy in an expose-all world and miss her inno-*
> *cence in a country filled with people eager to experience everything.*
> *We mourn the loss of Jacqueline Bouvier Kennedy Onassis' grace in*
> *this graceless society* (Stu Koblentz, *Time* Magazine, 6/20/94).

Webster defines *discretion* as the quality of being discerning or discriminat-
ing. Discretion springs from prudence, and often is interchangeable with it.
A discreet woman is careful about what she does and says. Likewise, one of
the Hebrew definitions of the word that is translated *discretion* is "taste." A
lady knows what is in good taste. My mother always taught her three daughters that a lady doesn't wear too much make-up, show too much of her body,
use vulgar language, chew gum in public, or go out without a girdle! (We've
skipped the last one, but tried to keep the rest!) However, discretion goes
deeper than this. For it is possible for a woman to win favor with the world
because she has grace and elegance, and yet not win favor with God. A dis-
tinguishing quality of discretion in *Webster's Dictionary* is: "the act of sepa-
rating, the state or quality of being separate or distinct." As Christians, we
are told to remember that we are "a chosen people, a royal priesthood, a
holy nation, a people belonging to God" (1 Peter 2:9). And women are
exhorted to behave as is "appropriate for women who profess to worship
God" (1 Tim. 2:10). This kind of behavior begins in the heart, with a surren-
der to God, and is developed through abiding in Christ and His Word.

WARMUP

Go around your circle, giving women the freedom to pass, and have each
woman share something their mother, grandmother, or other woman they
respected taught them about being a lady.

If new women have joined your group, introduce them and have them tell a
little about themselves.

SCRIPTURE STUDY
DAY I
. . . .

The Loveliness of Discretion

Review the introduction.

1. Solomon described his bride as being "like a lily among thorns" (Song
   2:2). Can you think of a contemporary woman who exemplifies this kind
   of striking loveliness—who is beautiful because she has poise and integrity? (Try to choose someone the others in the group would know.)

Who is she and why do you admire her?

Memorize the following proverb.

> *Like a gold ring in a pig's snout is a beautiful woman who shows
> no discretion* (Prov. 11:22).

2. Read Proverbs 11.

A. What proverbs particularly stand out to you at this time in your life
and why?

B. One aspect of discretion is to keep confidences. What is the contrast
in Proverbs 11:13?

C. What do you think Proverbs 11:22 means?

D. Can you give some examples of how a lovely woman's image can be
ruined by her words or behavior?

DAY 2

*A Woman of Discretion Embraces
Her Identity as a Woman*

In *Let Me Be a Woman* (Tyndale), Elisabeth Elliot tells how she and her husband prayed for a son, but were given a daughter. Elisabeth could see her husband's face when the doctor said, "It's a girl." Jim smiled at his wife and said at once, "Her name is Valerie." When Valerie became a young woman, her mother wrote to her:

> *We sometimes hear the expression "the accident of sex," as though
> one's being a man or a woman were a triviality. It is our nature. It is
> the modality under which we live all our lives; it is what you and I are
> called to be—called by God, this God who is in charge. It is our
> destiny, planned, ordained, fulfilled by an all-wise, all-powerful, all-
> loving Lord.*

The central theme of 1 Peter is that we are called for a purpose, and that purpose is to glorify God. Peter urges us to understand our identity as Christians, that we are set apart to be holy. He also has special additional insights from God for women. And though these insights are in the context of marriage, the qualities are applicable to single women as well. All women are to behave with purity and reverence, and though single women do not have a husband to whom they should submit, still, all believers are exhorted to live in submission to one another.

Read 1 Peter 3:1–6.

3. What specific instructions does Peter give to women who are married to unbelievers?

4. Contemplate each of the following phrases, looking at them in additional translations for more insight. For each word or phrase, give an example of a behavior which would demonstrate this quality.

■ Purity

■ Reverence

■ Unfading beauty of a gentle and quiet spirit

In your personal quiet time, sing "For the Beauty of the Earth" (p. 116). Gentleness and contentment springs from a worshipful and thankful heart.

5. Describe how God feels about a woman who has the above characteristics (v. 4).

6. How did Sarah show respect for Abraham? If you are married, how do you show respect for your husband?

7. Read Proverbs 12.
   A. What proverbs stand out to you at this time and why?

   B. How could embracing the truth of Proverbs 12:1 and 12:15 help you to grow in discretion?

C. What word pictures are used in Proverbs 12:4 to describe a wife of discretion and a wife of indiscretion?

D. How might a wife "shame" her husband?

E. What is the contrast in Proverbs 12:18?

F. Is there an application God is impressing on your heart from Proverbs 12?

DAY 3

A Woman of Discretion Avoids Excesses

Temperance, or moderation, is the characteristic that recognizes that God's good gifts can be abused and ruined. It is intriguing to me that it has often been women who have carried the baton of temperance in our society. As guardians of the home, perhaps women have been the first to see the threat of intemperance to the family. For example, women fought against the legalization of alcohol with "The Women's Christian Temperance Union." Sister organizations of a more contemporary flavor have sprung up to fight the abuse of sex as seen in pornography, TV, and rock music. Food, sex, conversation, and material blessings are all good gifts but must be tempered with wisdom. A woman of discretion guards against excesses in her life and allows her life to shine as a light to a society which is destroying itself through intemperance.

8. In each of the following proverbs, the phrase "too much" indicates an area where we should exercise moderation. Define the area where we are to guard against excess and then put the proverb in your own words.

A. *A gossip destroys a confidence; so avoid a man who talks too much* (Prov. 20:19).

B. *Do not join those who drink too much wine or gorge themselves on meat* (Prov. 23:20).

C. *Seldom set foot in your neighbor's house—too much of you, and he will hate you* (Prov. 25:17).

D. *It is not good to eat too much honey, nor is it honorable to seek one's own honor* (Prov. 25:27).

E. *Two things I ask of you, O LORD . . . give me neither poverty nor riches, but give me only my daily bread. Otherwise, I may have too much and disown you and say, "Who is the LORD?" Or I may become poor and steal, and so dishonor the name of my God* (Prov. 30:7–9).

9. Which of the above proverbs speaks most loudly to you? Why?

Review your memory verse.

DAY 4

A Woman of Discretion Is Cautious in Friendship

Our friends have an enormous influence on our lives. A wise woman is discreet in choosing who will be her closest friends. If our closest friends are weak, we will be as well. If we choose women who challenge us by their walk, their wisdom, and their truthful counsel, we will become like them.

There are enough warnings about the fool in Proverbs that we will take time today to consider how to recognize a fool. There is a difference between being foolish and a fool. Children are foolish (foolishness is bound up in the heart of a child) and all of us are foolish at times. But a fool is always foolish and will not change, because one of the prime characteristics of a fool is that he is always right. A discreet woman recognizes a fool and therefore keeps her distance.

My friend Jan Silvious, to whom this guide is dedicated, has had a dramatic impact on many lives, including my own, with her classic book, *Fool-Proofing Your Life*. Her study of Proverbs helped her to recognize a fool. Since then she has counseled many who are up close and personal with a fool—a parent, child, friend, or mate. Jan's counsel was instrumental in rescuing a daughter from an abusive relationship. However, if we had been wiser, we might have recognized the red flags before she became entangled in that relationship. We could have spared her great harm. Hopefully, this lesson will help you and your loved ones to be more discrete in avoiding fools such as boyfriends, mates, or close friends.

Fools can be charming, they can even be religious, yet in their hearts they say there is no God (Ps. 14:1). King Saul certainly was both charming and religious, yet his behavior continually exemplified that of a fool. He would be remorseful, but never truly repentant. He was hot-tempered and even murderous, he was given to many words, and many were insincere—designed to get his own way. A fool is all about himself, and a fool will destroy you if you walk closely with him.

> *He who walks with wise men will be wise,*
> *But the companion of fools will suffer harm* (Prov. 13:20 NAS).

Not only will we suffer harm if we make a fool a close friend, we will become like him, for we become like the people with whom we spend a lot of time.

> *Do not make friends with a hot-tempered man,*
> *do not associate with one easily angered,*
> *or you may learn his ways*
> *and get yourself ensnared* (Prov. 22:24–25).

10. Read Proverbs 13.

   A. Select one or two proverbs that impress you at this time in your life and explain why.

   B. What contrast is found in Proverbs 13:20?

   C. What will happen to you, according to Proverbs 13:20, if you marry a fool or choose a fool for a close friend?

11. The following proverbs give characteristics of a fool. Describe each, remembering it should be a red flag for a woman of discretion.

■ Proverbs 12:15a

This is a key. Because a fool is always right, he has no need to repent. This is what makes him so impervious to change. His plumbline is not the Scripture or this wisdom of the wise, but his own eyes.

■ Proverbs 14:16

■ Proverbs 18:2

■ Proverbs 20:3

■ Proverbs 26:11

■ Proverbs 28:26

■ Proverbs 29:11

12. Summarize how you might discern if someone may be a fool.

Review your memory passage.

DAY 5

Indiscreet Women

There is a warning in Scripture that is given uniquely to women, and since it is repeated, it is worthy of consideration.

13. Read Isaiah 3:13–24.

   A. Why is the Lord entering into judgment with His people? (Isaiah 3:13–15)

   B. What contrast is given in verse 16?

   C. How will the Lord judge them (Isaiah 3:17–24)?

   D. What heart attitude do these women have?

14. In contrast to the women of Zion, how does the Proverbs 31 woman behave? (See Prov. 31:20–22.)

15. Read 1 Peter 3:3–4. How are we to make ourselves beautiful?

16. How are women exhorted in 1 Timothy 2:9–10?

None of these passages teach that women cannot wear lovely clothes or care about their outward appearance. The woman of Proverbs 31 was adorned beautifully in fine linen and purple. But these passages repeatedly teach that inward beauty is what truly makes a woman beautiful in God's sight, and is a beauty that will not fade.

17. If you were to summarize what makes a woman beautiful from the above passages, what would it be? Do you think you really believe this? Explain.

18. In terms of outward appearance, what do the above passages teach about indiscretion in beauty?

19. In summary, describe a woman of discretion. What lesson has God particularly impressed on your heart?

PRAYER TIME

One effective way to pray in God's will is to pray through Scripture. Pair off in twos and pray through 1 Peter 3:2–4 for one another. For example, if I were paired with Lisa, a young single, I might pray:

Father, I pray for reverence for You to grow in Lisa's heart. Help her to draw near to You and keep Your holiness in mind. Keep her thoughts and actions pure. Help her to trust You with her fears—of her upcoming exam, of her desire to be married, of her dwindling finances. Fill her with the quiet beauty that comes from trusting You.

Prayers & Praises

_____

_____

_____

_____

_____

_____

_____

_____

_____

_____

_____

_____

_____

_____

Five

She Is Prudent
Zeresh/Abigail

P rudence" is such an old-fashioned word, and somehow, it has had connotations for me of being strait-laced, rigid, and prune-faced. I thought of a woman who lived her life by negatives: no movies, no make-up, no fun! But that is a distortion, for it is actually a positive word, for a prudent woman is one who takes action on the basis of wisdom. She prepares, plans, and prospers. I love it that we will look at Abigail, my heroine, for she surely did all three.

When Lemuel's mother gave him guidelines on what to look for in a woman of value, prudence was near the top of her list. A pretty playmate could ruin him! In her book, *The Complete Woman*, Patricia Gundry explains that while it may seem unromantic to look for a wife who knows how to handle responsibility and money wisely, many men would be much less stressed had they allowed their heads as well as their hearts to help them choose life partners. A wise man watches to see how a woman handles her finances, her housekeeping, and her temper. And he prays for a godly, loving, and prudent wife, for God says:

> *Houses and wealth are inherited from parents, but a prudent wife*
> *is from the LORD* (Prov. 19:14).

One possible meaning in the above proverb is that an imprudent wife may squander away any wealth that a man has inherited, but a prudent wife helps him to handle his money wisely. I interviewed one such wife recently, who is also the mother of seven sons. Cindy Sutphin told me the following story:

> *Seven years ago we were $10,000 in debt and not tithing. Under conviction, I prayed for wisdom and the Lord gave me a plan: If we moved to a less expensive home in the country, we could obey the Lord in the area of finances. When I suggested this to my husband Mark, he agreed—because the Lord had been dealing with him too! Not only were we able to pay off our debt and practice tithing, but we were richly blessed by our life in the country. During this time Mark realized that our love of the outdoors made us and our seven sons a perfect fit for a camping ministry. Today Mark is at Grace College of the Bible preparing for just such a ministry!*

Whether we are single or married, prudence is a characteristic which God values and which we should seek to cultivate. Prudence is wisdom that results in wise choices with money, with time, and with people.

WARMUP

Lemuel's mother advised him on how to find a prudent wife. If you had a son, share one red flag you would tell him to watch for, or one clear sign that she might be a treasure.

Ask for volunteers to recite the proverbs you've memorized so far.

SCRIPTURE STUDY
DAY 1

The Prudent Woman Considers Her Steps

Memorize the following:

> *Houses and wealth are inherited from parents, but a prudent wife is from the LORD* (Prov. 19:14).

Proverbs 14:8a says: "The wisdom of the prudent is to give thought to their ways." Susannah Wesley echoed this thought when she warned:

> *Do not live like the rest of mankind, who pass through the world like straws upon a river, which are carried which way the stream or wind drives them.*

1. Make a list of the three most important things you wish to accomplish with your life. What are you doing to accomplish these goals? How could you be more prudent?

Action Assignment

What are the most important things you wish to accomplish today? Prioritize and plan your schedule so that the most important things will be accomplished.

2. Read Proverbs 14.

A. What proverbs from this chapter stand out to you at this time in your life and why?

B. How does Proverbs 14:1 describe a prudent wife?

C. Give examples of "building" and "tearing down."

D. What quality of prudence do you find in Proverbs 14:8? How could you do this more habitually each day?

E. What does a simple person do that a prudent person avoids? (Prov. 14:15) How could this apply to you?

F. What contrast is given in verse 22? How could you apply this even today?

G. What two blessings of fearing the Lord are found in verse 26?

H. What contrast is given in verse 30?

Modern medicine has discovered what the Scriptures taught long ago. There is a relationship between the mind and the body.

DAY 2

....

The Prudent Woman Plans Ahead

3. How did yesterday's Action Assignment affect your day?

Life simply happens to the imprudent. They don't think ahead to eternity, let alone to the next month. They purchase things impulsively, say whatever comes into their head, and lack caution in explosive situations. The prudent behave very differently.

4. Explain how the prudent behave in each of the following passages. Record also any personal applications.

> *A prudent man is reluctant to display his knowledge, but the heart of (self-confident) fools proclaims their folly* (Prov. 12:23 AMP).

> *The prudent see danger and take refuge, but the simple keep going and suffer for it* (Prov. 27:12).

> *She sees that her trading is profitable, and her lamp does not go out at night* (Prov. 31:18).

"Her lamp does not go out at night" simply means that she has remembered to buy sufficient oil for her lamp. The imprudent can identify with Erma Bombeck who tells her neighbors that if they need anything at the grocery store to let her know, because she goes every two hours!

5. How have you planned ahead to try to avoid:

■ Overspending

■ Dying prematurely from cancer, heart disease, etc.

■ Raising a fool

■ Being conformed to the world

■ Regrets in eternity

6. Read Proverbs 15:1–17

   A. What proverbs stand out to you and why?

   B. What advice does Proverbs 15:1 give? Have you found this to be helpful? If so, explain.

   C. What does Proverbs 15:17 mean? See also Proverbs 17:1. How might you apply these?

Spend some time on your memory passage.

DAY 3

She Handles Volatile Situations Prudently

When my friend Lee came to Christ, her old friends were critical of her new faith. At a coffee, I listened as they told her that she'd "become a fanatic" and was "taking the Bible too literally." Lee listened quietly, respectfully.

> *"All I know," Lee said sincerely, "is that Jesus has changed my life." After the coffee, she kept loving those friends and finding ways to minister to their needs. In time, a few came to her Bible study and two came to know Christ. A prudent woman doesn't lose her cool! Thoughtfully, prayerfully, she determines how God would have her resolve conflict, and then she acts, trusting God to be with her.*

7. What wisdom do each of the following proverbs give you in dealing with people?

■ Proverbs 12:16

■ Proverbs 15:5

■ Proverbs 16:7

8. Read Proverbs 15:18–33.

   A. What proverbs spoke to you from the above passage and why?

   B. We often bring trouble to our own lives. How can this be seen in the following:

■ Proverbs 15:19a

■ Proverbs 15:22a

■ Proverbs 15:27a

9. Is God speaking to you through any of the above? If so, how?

DAY 4

Zeresh, An Imprudent Woman

Read Esther 5:9–14.

10. How did Zeresh, Haman's wife, respond when he came home petulant about Mordecai's refusal to bow down to him?

Read Esther 7.

11. How did Zeresh's response to Haman backfire?

Can you think of a time when your lack of prudence caused suffering for you or those close to you? If so, what is God teaching you?

Keeping cool is important in volatile situations. However, a prudent woman needs to do more than refrain from losing her temper. She needs a plan that is inspired by the Spirit of God. Esther exemplified this—she spent three days fasting before she approached her volatile husband. God gave her incredible wisdom, timing, and power.

12. If you have drawn upon God's wisdom in a time of fasting and prayer before moving ahead in an important area, share something about it.

13. Read Proverbs 16

    A. What proverbs stood out to you from this chapter and why?

    B. What encouraging counsel is in Proverbs 16:7? How might this guide you when people are being very critical of you?

DAY 5 ....

Abigail, an Example of Prudence

Author Brenda Wilbee, in *Taming the Dragons,* gives insight on how women have creatively resolved conflict in their lives. She says that often Christian women are discouraged from taking action, but instead are told to wait for rescue. And yet when we look at the prudent women in Scripture, we see they asked God for a plan, took action, and experienced victory. Consider Esther, Jochebed, Hannah, Deborah, and Abigail! Because of our study of the fool, and how difficult it is if you are up close and personal with one, I am choosing Abigail, who was commended by David for her prudence, and certainly models for us how to deal with a fool.

Read 1 Samuel 25:1–17.

14. In the above passage, how is Abigail described? How is her husband Nabal described?

15. How had David and his men been helpful to Nabal and his men in the past? Note everything you can about their behavior.

How did Nabal respond to the request? Note everything you can about his behavior.

16. Describe the conflict Abigail faced as described to her by the servant.

Read 1 Samuel 25:18–35.

Brenda Wilbee describes Abigail's method as "naming and taming conflict."

"My Lord, pay no attention to that wicked man Nabal," she said, cutting to the quick of the conflict by naming the truth. "He is just like his name—his name is Fool, and folly goes with him."

What? Call your husband a fool? . . . What wife has the right to malign her husband, for whatever reason?

But Abigail was not maligning anyone. "Please," she said to David, still bowed before him. "Forgive Nabal's offense."

She was not out to create trouble, but to resolve it. . . . Shrewd yet innocent, Abigail saw and named the deepest level of the dilemma, her husband's folly—and then went on to seek creative alternatives, and the dragon was transformed (Brenda Wilbee, *Taming the Dragons*, Harper-Collins).

17. Find ways that Abigail creatively "tamed the dragon" of David's anger. What principles do you see which could be helpful to you?

18. Are you experiencing a challenge in your life? Can you learn anything from Abigail that might help? If so, what?

I regret that there were times in my younger years when I failed to give prudent counsel to women in abusive relationships. When a woman would come to me and tell me that her marriage was in trouble, I would always counsel her to stay with her husband, but to get help. Now I realize that, often, if she stays, he won't get help. Instead, she enables his bad behavior. If there are signs of abuse (emotional, physical, sexual) then the more prudent counsel would be to tell her to separate from her husband, to insist he get help, and not to return until there is real evidence of a changed life. If he is not a fool, he may very well go for help for his addictions, abuse, or unfaithfulness. If he is a fool, then he will refuse, for he feels he is always right and does not need counsel. He may then abandon her, be unfaithful to her, or divorce her. Yet to stay with an abusive man is unwise. She is hurting him, herself, and her children. If she separates, she at least has hope for her marriage, for he may get help. Abigail didn't allow Nabal to ruin lives. Though it took great courage, she planned good and acted on it. God blessed and intervened.

19. Why may it seem like the easier road to stay with an abusive man and support his folly? How would you counsel a woman in this situation?

Two helpful resources are *Fool-Proofing Your Life* by Jan Silvious and *Boundaries* by Henry Cloud and John Townsend. Settingcaptivesfree.com also provides support for people in addictive behaviors such as gambling, pornography, and alcoholism.

Read 1 Samuel 25:36–42.

20. Describe what happened to Nabal, Abigail, and David.

21. How does Abigail exemplify prudence?

PRAYER TIME

Pray conversationally for one another's challenges. Lift up your own challenge and allow the others to support you, asking God for a plan, for courage, and for success. Close by singing "Turn Your Eyes Upon Jesus" (p. 117).

Prayers & Praises

_____

_____

_____

_____

_____

_____

_____

_____

_____

_____

_____

_____

_____

_____

_____

Six

She Honors Her Husband
Rebekah/Elizabeth

My husband and I came to Christ early in our marriage, but as a baby Christian, I failed to truly honor my husband. His hours in medical training were long, and I nagged him about it like the woman in Proverbs who is compared to the "drip, drip, drip" of a faucet! But through the Scriptures, a growing reverence for the Lord, and godly women who mentored me, my attitude and behavior toward Steve changed. As I sought to show my husband honor, as I prayed for him, as I sought to be supportive of his goals as a physician, wonderful things occurred in our marriage. He was so grateful for the change in my behavior that he did all he could to honor me. We spent time each day in intimate conversation, he gave me foot-rubs every night, he prayed over me, he supported my time away in ministry sacrificially, and our hearts were filled with joyful anticipation each evening when we would be reunited.

WARMUP

Go around the circle, asking women to share one example of a way a woman might show her husband honor or fail to show him honor. Pair off and review your memory verses.

SCRIPTURE STUDY

DAY 1

She Brings Him Good All the Days of Her Life

Memorize the following passage.

> *A wife of noble character who can find? She is worth far more than rubies. Her husband has full confidence in her and lacks nothing of value. She brings him good, not harm, all the days of her life* (Prov. 31:10–12).

1. Meditate on this passage and write down observations. Look for key words, comparisons, contrasts, cause and effect, questions, and tone. Write down everything you find.

2. Write down a few principles you find in this passage. Do you see an application for yourself? What is it?

> The book of Proverbs as a whole takes a view of marriage that remains proverbial to this day: that there is nothing in the world worse than a bad marriage, and at the same time nothing better than a good one (Mike Mason, *The Mystery of Marriage*, Multnomah, p. 24).

3. Read Proverbs 17.

   A. What proverbs stood out to you and why?

   B. What does Proverbs 17:17 teach?

   C. If you are married, how can you better love your husband when he is down? When he is facing adversity? If you are single, apply this to a good friend.

DAY 2

. . . .

Women Who Bring Men Harm

Read Proverbs 31:1–3.

4. Using your imagination, describe the kind of woman who could "ruin a king" (or a man).

5. The following Proverbs warn about women who bring harm to their husbands and family. Describe each and give an example of how her behavior might dishonor her husband.

■ Proverbs 2:16–17

■ Proverbs 12:4b

■ Proverbs 14:1

■ Proverbs 21:9

■ Proverbs 27:15

6. If you are a wife, how do you show your husband honor?

Action Assignment

Get a man's point of view. Ask a man whom you respect what kind of woman he thinks a man should avoid when choosing a wife. Then show him the above proverbs. Ask him which one he would most severely warn his son against, if he had a son of marrying age. Record his comments below.

7. Did you learn anything from the Action Assignment? If so, what?

8. Read Proverbs 18.

A. What proverbs stand out to you from this chapter and why?

B. "The name of the LORD" signifies the attributes of God and His ability to protect. What does Proverbs 18:10 teach?

C. How might you apply the above to a problem you are facing?

Review your memory work.

DAY 3

Elizabeth, A Woman with a Clear Conscience

Sheila is a godly pastor's wife. At a bridal shower, she gave a devotional on getting along with your husband! Gently, she shared.

> *Early on in our marriage my husband and I discovered that if there was trouble between us, there was usually something troubling our relationship with the Lord. So we would each get alone with the Lord and seek to clear up our relationship with Him. Then we found that our relationship with each other cleared up as well.*

How I agree! And I believe that one of the reasons that the marriage of Zechariah and Elizabeth was so sound was because they each made sure their relationship with the Lord was good. For we are told:

> *Together they lived honorably before God, careful in keeping to the ways of the commandments and enjoying a clear conscience before God* (Luke 1:6, MSG).

9. Describe the way a person must live in order to enjoy a clear conscience before God.

Do you agree that a clear conscience before God makes you a better wife? (a better friend?) Why or why not?

Read Luke 1:7.

10. Elizabeth had to live with the disappointment of barrenness, and yet she continued to love, trust, and obey God. Why do you think she responded that way?

I believe that Elizabeth knew God loved her. In your quiet time, sing the "Cares Chorus" (pp. 118-119).

11. Read Proverbs 19.

A. What proverbs stood out to you and why?

B. To what is a quarrelsome wife compared in verse 13? How could you avoid being like this?

C. What does verse 17 teach?

DAY 4

Elizabeth, An Encouraging Life Partner

Read Luke 1:8–25. (In your group discussion, read aloud only verses 18, 24–25.)

12. Contrast the reactions of Elizabeth and Zechariah to Gabriel's news.

Elizabeth evidently had no problems in believing the fantastic promise, even though she had not received it as her husband had, directly from God through a godly messenger. . . . If Elizabeth did react more spiritually than her husband to the news, there is no evidence of any self-exaltation. Nor did she look down on him. She didn't move him down in order to move herself up. Rather, she responded like a good wife who accepts weakness in her life-partner (Gien Karssen, *Her Name is Woman*, NavPress, p. 145).

13. Do you agree that it is important to accept weakness in your life-partner? Why or why not?

Read Luke 1:39–45.

14. What can you learn from Elizabeth's example of encouraging others spiritually?

How might a woman apply this to encouraging her husband spiritually?

Review all your memory passages.

DAY 5

Rebekah, Who with Her Own Hands, Destroyed Her Home

Rebekah was a believer and her marriage to Isaac began with great promise (Gen. 24). Yet, later in the marriage we see her tearing down her home with her own hands.

Read Genesis 27 on your own.

15. Summarize the events of the chapter in a few sentences.

16. List a few of the consequences of Rebekah's behavior for her marriage, her relationship with her sons, and their relationship with each other.

Rebekah failed to honor her husband, yet, as long as there is life, there is hope. Author and counselor Gary Smalley has said: "The secret to renewing any strained relationship is honor" (*If Only He Knew*, Zondervan, p. 4).

17. Rebekah's marriage to Isaac began with great hope as she trusted God. What do you think happened?

Do you find any warning for yourself in this story? If so, what?

18. Read Proverbs 20.

   A. What proverbs stood out to you and why?

   B. What truth is taught in verse 9? How could you respond to this throughout the day so that you can be "blameless" like Elizabeth?

PRAYER TIME

Pray in twos or conversationally, using your memory verse to guide you for part of your prayer time. Close by singing "Turn Your Eyes Upon Jesus" (p. 117).

Prayers & Praises

Seven

She Finds Her Work to Be a Joy
The Idle Widows/ The Diligent Widows

One of the most satisfying aspects of life is work! As a homemaker, I find it immensely gratifying to see my family enjoying a home-cooked meal around a candlelit table. As a writer, I love the creative process: praying, researching, seeing ideas take shape, working with words. As a co-laborer with other believers, seeing an evangelistic Bible study which I've helped plant take off and change lives is more exciting to me than a trip to a South Sea Island. This gives life meaning! Whether in the home, the workplace, or in ministry—work is a blessing! It was part of God's plan before the Fall and should be good. Even when it is menial, it can still be good, because it is part of my life's offering to God. If it is not satisfying, I need an attitude change!

WARMUP

Go around, giving women the freedom to pass, and ask: Think about a recent time when your work in the home or ministry or the workplace gave you pleasure. What did you do and why did it give you joy?

SCRIPTURE STUDY

DAY 1
• •

Attitude Is Key

The Proverbs 31 woman can intimidate any of us, for she seems like super woman. It is helpful to know she is a composite picture of a bride, and it is lovely to see her as well as "the Bride of Christ." Rather than being overwhelmed by all she accomplishes, look at her attitude. What permeates the chapter is her attitude of eagerness, of strength, of absolute delight in planning, executing, and enjoying the fruit of her labor.

Memorize the following:
> *She watches over the affairs of her household and does not eat the bread of idleness* (Prov. 31:27).

1. Meditate on the following verses describing the Proverbs 31 woman. What insight can you glean in each about her attitude? (In your personal quiet time, work thoughtfully through these verses.)

■ verse 11

■ verse 13

■ verse 15

■ verse 16

■ verse 17

■ verse 18

■ verse 20

■ verse 21

■ verse 22

■ verse 25

■ verse 26

■ verse 27

■ verse 30

2. Summarize her attitude. What particularly impresses you?

Action Assignment

Is there a job in your home or workplace which needs to be done but you have been avoiding? Change your attitude and plan how and when you will accomplish it. What is your plan?

DAY 2
....

The Secret of a Positive Attitude toward Work

No matter what this 17th-century believer was doing, Brother Lawrence was offering it up to Christ, and his face radiated joy:

> *The Special Diets kitchen was often very busy, and usually under-staffed. The phone seemed to ring incessantly . . . but, in the busiest moments, with noise, heat and tempers getting a bit frayed at the edges, Laurie remained calm—and close to God. . . . He was serving God, and that would be best done by being calm, composed... and hard-working* (David Winter, *Closer Than a Brother*, Shaw, p. 160).

> *Whatever you do, work at it with all your heart, as working for the Lord, not for men, since you know that you will receive an inheritance from the Lord as a reward. It is the Lord Christ you are serving* (Col. 3:23–24).

3. Describe the attitude we should have according to the above passage.

> The Christian attitude toward work is truly revolutionary. Think what it would do to the economy and the entire fabric of life if the question were asked daily, in the kitchen, in the office, the schoolroom, the plant: "Who is your Master?" and the answer were given: "Christ is my Master, whose slave I am" (Elisabeth Elliot, *Discipline: The Glad Surrender,* Revell, pp. 132–33).

4. If you fully realized that you were serving Christ in your work, how do you think it would impact your attitude toward:

■ Work that is menial and routine

■ Times when others do not notice your efforts

■ Your boss

■ Fellow employees

■ Your salary

5. Read Proverbs 21.

   A. What proverbs particularly stand out to you and why?

   B. What do you discover about wise and unwise work according to the following proverbs? Meditate on each for your own life. The first one warns about being hasty—don't be hasty in your work of studying the Word.

■ Proverbs 21:5

■ Proverbs 21:15 and 17 (There is a contrast of work goals here.)

■ Proverbs 21:25–26

    C. What similar truth do you find in Proverbs 21:9 and Proverbs 21:19? Is there an application for your life?

Keep memorizing your passage.

DAY 3

She Is neither Slothful nor Deceived Concerning Work

Derek Kidner writes:

> The sluggard in Proverbs is a figure of tragic-comedy, with his sheer animal laziness (he is more than anchored to his bed; he is *hinged* to it, 26:14), his preposterous excuses ("there is a lion outside!" 22:13; 26:13) and his final helplessness (Derek Kidner, *Proverbs*, InterVarsity Press, p. 42).

Sloth can simply be laziness: excessive sleeping, sitting around in front of the TV every evening, or finding excuses to escape work. Not only will the sluggard not start or finish things, he begins to believe his own excuses. There is definitely an element of deceit in laziness. Our hearts are naturally deceitful, so we must continually ask God to search them. How easy it is, also, to substitute what we want to do for what God wants us to do and tell ourselves we are doing it for the Lord. Yet if we are working for pleasure, fame, or riches rather than to please God, we have been deceived. We *will* reap what we sow.

6. Read Proverbs 22.

    A. What proverbs particularly stand out to you and why?

B. Some work for pleasure, some for riches—what does Proverbs 22:1 teach? How could this apply to your work?

C. Not all work is good. Each of us will reap what we sow. What warning is given in Proverbs 22:8?

D. What warning is given to the employer in Proverbs 22:16?

7. What do you learn about the slothful person from the following word pictures or comparisons?

■ Proverbs 6:6–11

■ Proverbs 26:13–16

8. One Hebrew word which is translated *slothful* or *sluggard* has the connotation of deceit. What excuse does the lazy person give in Proverbs 22:13? What creative excuses have you given?

9. God says that the "heart is deceitful above all things, and desperately wicked" (Jer. 17:9, KJV). Often we do not know that we are deceiving ourselves, and our excuses seem valid. Think about some of the things God has called you to do but that you tend to avoid. What are those things?

In an article in *Leadership* (Spring 1994), John Ortberg points out that many lazy people are busy, for though sloth can be inactivity, it can also be "the failure to do what needs to be done when it needs to be done." God rejected Saul as king because Saul substituted activity for what God had called him to do (1 Sam. 15:1–23).

10. What jobs has God called you to do? How can you be sure you are not neglecting them?

11. If you are a mother, aunt, or grandmother, what is part of your God-given work according to:

■ Proverbs 22:6

■ Proverbs 22:15

We will look more at training children next week. It is common to be lazy in disciplining children when they are young, and the consequences for this are disastrous for parent and child.

12. The lazy person tends to be "wiser in his own conceit" (Prov. 26:16 KJV), and yet he or she is really "void of understanding" (Prov. 24:30 KJV) for sloth leads to trouble. List the consequence of sloth in each of the following and explain how it could be hard in your life.

■ Proverbs 10:26

■ Proverbs 12:24

■ Proverbs 13:4

■ Proverbs 15:19

■ Proverbs 20:13

■ Proverbs 24:30–34

DAY 4

Idle Women

In his first letter to Timothy, Paul gives guidelines for deciding which widows in the church were worthy of support and which were not. In part, these decisions were made on the basis of age and whether or not they had families, but also on the basis of whether their lifestyle was idle or diligent.

In your personal quiet time, sing some of the songs found in the back of this guide.

As an overview, read 1 Timothy 5:3–16.

13. Describe the characteristics of the women who were wasting their lives according to verses 6 and 13.

14. Why is it that idleness often leads to gossip or being busybodies? What warning do you see here for yourself?

15. We may not go "house to house" physically, but we may do it by cell phone or e-mail. What is a prudent and imprudent use of these means of communication?

16. What do you think Paul means when he says she "is dead even while she lives"? (See also Rev. 3:1.)

In contrast, examine the following verse.

> *I have been crucified with Christ and I no longer live, but Christ lives in me. The life I live in the body, I live by faith in the Son of God, who loved me and gave himself for me* (Gal. 2:20).

17. In the above verse, what is the secret of a vibrant and meaningful life?

> One of the things that will happen to you when you give yourself to Jesus as Lord of your life is that He will give you the strength to serve Him (Tom Osborne, Coach of the Nebraska Huskers, FCA Banquet, 11/15/94).

18. Read Proverbs 23

   A. What proverbs stand out to you right now and why?

   B. The three opening proverbs warn against social climbing. What warning is given in the following and why? How could each apply to you?

■ Proverbs 23:1–3

■ Proverbs 23:4–5

■ Proverbs 23:6–8

The miser may be as costly as the rich ruler. If he is currying favor with you to get something from you, be wary of the price! Derek Kidner says, "It takes away one's relish to have one's host doing mental arithmetic with each dish" (Derek Kidner, *Proverbs*, InterVarsity Press, p. 151). Sometimes it is the wiser course to gently refuse certain gifts, favors, or invitations from relatives or acquaintances. I run the other way, for example, when invited to a pyramid sales party. Too many of these companies (not all, but many) prey upon Christian women, telling them this is a way to make money easily at home (get rich quick!), dangling luxurious items before them. Some companies even counsel their "employees" to meet with friends under false pretenses, rather than truly being up front with them. The warnings of proverbs are as relevant today as they were in Solomon's day.

C. What warnings are given in verses 29–35?

If you are in bondage to alcoholism or another addiction, I recommend the website: settingcaptivesfree.com

Review your memory work.

DAY 5

Diligent Women

Paul commends the woman who "puts her hope in God and continues night and day to pray and to ask God for help" (1 Tim. 5:5). Not only will these actions give a woman the strength to be diligent, but it will give her the wisdom to do what God is calling her to do.

19. How are women who led valuable lives described in 1 Timothy 5:9–10?

Is God speaking to you through the above passage? If so, how?

20. Read Proverbs 24.

A. What proverbs stand out to you and why?

B. What does verse 27 advise? What does this mean?

21. What do you think you will remember about this lesson?

PRAYER TIME

Pray in twos or conversationally, using your memory verse to guide you for part of your prayer time. Close by singing the "Cares Chorus" (p. 118-119).

NEXT WEEK

If you have many young mothers in your group, divide Chapter 8 into two lessons, assigning Day 1 and Day 2 for next week.

Prayers & Praises

Eight

She Trains Her Children
Herodias/Eunice and Lois

Susannah Wesley bore nineteen children and raised two mighty men of God: John and Charles. Charles gave us some of our most beloved hymns, including "Hark the Herald Angels Sing" and "Christ the Lord Has Risen Today!" Susannah home-schooled her children and pulled her apron over her head for her own devotional hour with the Lord. Before Susannah died, John asked her to write down her philosophy of training young children. She wrote:

> *The children were always put into a regular method of living, in such things as they were capable of, from their birth; as in dressing, undressing, changing their linen. . . . When turned a year old (and some before), they were taught to fear the rod and to cry softly; by which means they escaped abundance of correction they might otherwise have had; and that most odious noise of the crying of children was rarely heard in the house. . . . They were never suffered to choose their meat, but always made to eat such things as were provided for the family. . . . In order to form the minds of children, the first thing to be done is to conquer their will and bring them to an obedient temper. . . . The children of this family were taught, as soon as they could speak, the Lord's Prayer . . . and some portion of Scripture, as their memories could bear. . . . They were quickly made to understand they might have nothing they cried for and instructed to speak handsomely for what they wanted (The Journal of John Wesley,* Moody, pp. 104–107).

WARMUP

Go around the circle, asking women to share one thing from Susannah Wesley's example that impresses them. As a review, ask volunteers to share their memory work of Proverbs 31:26–30.

SCRIPTURE STUDY

DAY I

. . . .

Faithful Instruction Is on Her Tongue

Memorize the following passage.

> *Her children arise and call her blessed; her husband also, and he praised her: "Many women do noble things, but you surpass them all"* (Prov. 31:28–29).

1. John and Charles Wesley praised their mother, Susannah. What do you imagine were some of the qualities for which they were most thankful?

Read Deuteronomy 6:6–9.

2. What similarities do you see between this passage and Proverbs 31:26–27?

If you are a mother, how are you seizing opportunities to faithfully instruct your children?

Action Assignment

An often fatal mistake made by Christian parents is to delegate the discipling of their children to the church. Church activities are important, but God has called parents to disciple their children all through the day. If you have children at home, seize at least one opportunity daily to disciple your children. (Act out a Bible story, visit a shut-in, pray together, sing praises together, memorize and discuss a proverb at dinner, etc.) Then list what you did.

Not only must faithful instruction be on our tongues, but faithful encouragement. If you do not have a positive relationship with your children, they will be deaf to your instruction. Author Mike Yorky put it like this: "Rules are important, but relationship is the bulls-eye." Proverbs 25 gives us some wonderful counsel for faithful encouragement.

3. Read Proverbs 25.

A. What proverbs stood out to you and why?

B. Proverbs 25:11–12 may apply to gentle rebuke. There is an effective and ineffective way to rebuke. What word pictures are used to describe a "word fitly spoken?" (vv. 11–12 KJV) Can you think of an illustration of this?

Kindness and clarity with children help a word to be fitly spoken. Always be kind, and never demean their character. A good "trainer" uses not just a negative but a positive. (See Eph. 5:25–32.) God does this with His children, and so should we with ours. For example, when a child whines for more food, say, "Please don't whine, but ask handsomely for the rolls." Then teach them precisely: "Mother, could you please pass the rolls?" When they do well, praise them.

C. What is a broken promise compared to in verse 9-10?

As a mother, if you make a promise to your child, whether it is a trip to the park or a bedtime story, keep your word. You are modeling integrity or the lack of it.

D. What warning is in verse 24? How could this apply to parenting as well as to marriage?

I have found it is better to set fewer boundaries and keep them than to set many and fail. Be diligent to keep them when they are young and they will grow to give you rest. If you set too many and cannot keep them, you will nag them all of their lives and no one will have rest. Sit down with your husband and determine what is really important and how you will reinforce it.

DAY 2

She Trains Her Children to Respect and Obey Authority

Review your memory passage.

As a baby Christian with two little boys, I was a permissive mother who was reluctant to discipline. A Christian teacher called Steve and me in for a conference when our firstborn son went to school. Gently, this godly older woman told us:

> *The happiest children are children who have been trained to respect authority. It's not too late for you to train your son. Go to him, ask his forgiveness, and tell him there will be a change. You and your husband must define the boundaries and paddle your son when he defies you. He will soon learn to respect you, the paddlings will become rare, and there will be hope for his future.*

Today our five grown children are all walking with the Lord—in large part, I am convinced, because we helped them to respect and obey authority.

4. Read the following proverbs and write down the principle which is being taught in each:

■ Proverbs 13:24

■ Proverbs 19:18

■ Proverbs 29:17

5. If you are an older mother and have experienced the truth of the above proverbs, share something with the younger mothers to encourage them.

6. Based on the above proverbs, what overriding principle do you see? Do you see an application for your life?

Many secular child psychologists are opposed to spanking, calling it child abuse. It is true that approaching a spanking in anger can be abusive. For this reason, as a young mom, I refused to spank. An author who helped me to see my error was Larry Christensen. In *The Christian Family* (Bethany), he explains that the world often spanks in anger, which is abusive, but a godly parent spanks with regret, to help his child learn to obey. Christensen says "the whole atmosphere is different and the children sense it at once."

Christensen also warns against provoking a child to wrath (Eph. 6:4). Don't, he warns:

(1) Punish them for childish irresponsibility (Dr. Dobson agrees—punish only for defiance).

(2) Set too many rules! Christensen says: "Many rules, many infractions."

(3) Elect a long, drawn out punishment (such as grounding them for a week).

(4) Allow them to show you disrespect (enforce the rules you've set down consistently).

Spanking is not the only way to discipline, and sometimes other forms are wise. For example, if a child breaks a rule about television or video games, cover the set with a sheet for a day. Have the child write an essay explaining how he disobeyed, why he should obey, and how he will respond next time. But the spanking of young children is advised in Scripture, and who are we to disagree with God?

As we put Christensen's wisdom into practice, our little boys became happier, more secure. They always preferred spankings to other forms of discipline—for then it was dealt with, and over. We hugged them, loved them, and put it in the past. Out of respect for their bodies, we found other forms of discipline in adolescence—though very little was needed.

7. Read Proverbs 26.

A. What proverbs stood out to you and why?

B. What does Proverbs 26:4 teach? What does Proverbs 26:5 teach? What does this opposing counsel teach you about proverbs?

Proverbs are not promises but general truths. Sometimes, it is wiser not to answer a fool and other times it is better to answer him. R. C. Sproul says we have that same happening in common proverbs. Sometimes he who hesitates is lost, other times we must look before we leap. The Holy Spirit must guide us on which course is wiser in each circumstance. By putting the above proverbs side by side, God helps us to understand something of the nature of a proverb.

    C. A fool is a fool spiritually, having never learned to fear God or respect His authority. He suffers for being this way. How can this be seen in verse 11?

Note: If you have many young mothers in your group and have decided to divide Chapter 8 into two lessons, you may want to stop here the first week.

DAY 3

She Trains through Positive Reinforcement

It is important to discipline disrespectful behavior. However, a mother who trains only through chastisement may discourage the spirit of her child and pave the way for future rebellion. Like sun and rain to a wilting flower are the words of praise and small rewards to a growing child.

> *The wise in heart are called discerning, and pleasant words promote instruction* (Prov. 16:21).

> *Pleasant words are a honeycomb, sweet to the soul and healing to the bones* (Prov. 16:24).

8. What do you learn from the above proverbs about pleasant words?

Is there an application to your life?

Gifts, or as it is sometimes translated, "bribes" can be used for evil or for good. When they are used to pervert justice, as in Proverbs 17:23, God condemns them. However, they can also be used to encourage good behavior. I agree with Dr. Dobson who encourages charts with stickers for good behavior such as a clean room, faithful practicing on the piano, well-done chores, and reading good books. Those stickers eventually can be turned in for small prizes. I was always amazed at the power of stickers in helping children to develop good habits with a cheerful heart. My husband used to say that he was going to put the following proverb on my tombstone, claiming it has been my life verse as a mother of five:

> *A gift is as a precious stone in the eyes of him that hath it:*
> *whithersoever it turneth, it prospereth* (Prov. 17:8 KJV).

9. What do you learn from the above proverb? Is there an application for your life?

Perhaps the most famous proverb concerning training children is Proverbs 22:6:

> *Train a child in the way he should go, and when he is old he will*
> *not turn from it.*

10. What principle is in the above verse? Is there an application for your life?

There has been much written by experts on the above proverb. Dr. John White in *Parents in Pain* reminds us that proverbs are generalities, not promises. Therefore, if you do all you can to raise a child to love the Lord, to respect authority, and to be a kind person—he probably will be, but there are exceptions, and good parents have been known to have rebellious children. Dr. James Dobson (*The New Dare to Discipline*) talks about the importance of understanding your child's particular bent ("the way he should go") and encouraging him in the way of his spiritual gifts, talents, and general strengths. Counselor Jay Adams (*Competent to Counsel*) has a different, but intriguing, perspective on this verse. He feels it is a warning, rather than an encouragement. Literally, he says, it says "Train a child after the manner of his way"—in other words, if you train a child to believe he can have his own way, which is rebellious and foolish, when he is old, he will continue to want his own way, and not God's way. However, whether it is a warning or an encouragement, it is clear we are to train our children when they are young to love and serve God!

Review your memory work.

DAY 4

A Foolish Mother: Herodias
A Foolish Father: Eli

Herodias was not a believer, but Eli was. It is possible to be a believer and still be a poor parent. Eli had many good qualities, yet he failed to restrain his sons. How careful we must be not to be so involved in ministering to others that we fail to minister to the ones God has clearly given us.

11. Read Proverbs 27

   A. What proverbs stand out to you and why?

   B. What similar truths are in Proverbs 27:5–6?

   C. What gives delight according to Proverbs 27:9?

I am so thankful for friends who give me earnest or hearty counsel. These are the friends who, when I come to them for counsel, pray about it and seek God, and then counsel me in a spirit of genuine love and wisdom. How I urge young mothers to go to wise older mothers for this kind of counsel in raising their children.

   D. What does Proverbs 27:10 teach?

Read Mark 6:14–29. (In your group, read only verses 22–29.)
12. What do you learn about the character of Herodias from this passage?

13. How was Salome, her daughter, like her?

What negative attitudes might you be passing on to the next generation?

Read 1 Samuel 2:12–25.
14. Describe the behavior and attitude of Eli's sons.

Read 1 Samuel 2:27—3:14.

15. What prophecies were given to Eli? How did Eli fail as a father?

Why do you think Eli failed to restrain his sons when they were young? What are some reasons parents fail to restrain their children?

DAY 5

Mothers Who Discipled Their Children: Lois and Eunice

Review your memory passage.

Read 2 Timothy 1:5.

16. What do you learn about Timothy? As you think over your life, would a child or grandchild watching you have seen times when you were trusting in God? If so, share one.

Read 2 Timothy 3:14–17.

17. What other things do you learn about Timothy's upbringing from this passage?

18. Practice explaining the Gospel (the Good News on how we can be forgiven and assured of heaven) so that a child could understand. (There's a visual explanation on pages 94–96.)

19. What have you learned about training your children that you think you will remember?

PRAYER TIME

Use Popcorn Prayer to lift up each woman. If she is a mother, pray particularly for her in that role. Close by singing the "Cares Chorus" (p. 118-119).

Prayers &
Praises

_____

_____

_____

_____

_____

_____

_____

_____

_____

_____

_____

_____

_____

_____

Nine

She Finds Favor
Jezebel/Mary, the Mother of Jesus

The woman of wisdom is obedient to God because she loves and fears Him—and not to gain favor. Still, she is blessed. One of the prevailing themes of the book of Proverbs is that blessings and honor abound on the righteous. This does not mean that we are free of trouble, but that God is with us in difficult times and blesses us in ways that those who don't obey Him can never know.

WARMUP

Go around, giving women the freedom to pass, and say: Share a specific way God has blessed you as you have endeavored to trust and obey Him.

SCRIPTURE STUDY

DAY 1

Her Works Endure

Perhaps the greatest blessing of all for a woman of wisdom is the knowledge that her life will bear lasting fruit, for those things that are done for Christ endure forever. She is storing up treasures in heaven. In addition, her memory on earth is blessed, and her example is carried on from generation to generation.

> *Linda Barry, who grew up in poverty in a "disintegrating" family, watched her neighbor and learned from her. She says that, as a little girl, she loved going to Mrs. Taylor's house because "even if it wasn't happening in her house, just being near it counted for something." One day Linda sneaked over to Mrs. Taylor's at dawn:*

> *I stood on her porch knocking and knocking and knocking, weighing how much of a bother I was becoming against how badly I needed to see her. . . . When I told her my mom said I could eat with them, she laughed and pushed open the screen door....*

> *I'll never forget that morning, sitting at their table eating eggs and toast, watching them talk to each other and smile. How Mr. Taylor made a joke and Mrs. Taylor laughed. How she put her hand on his shoulder as she poured coffee and he leaned his face down to kiss it.*

> *And that was all I needed to see. I only needed to see it once to be able to believe for the rest of my life that happiness between two people can exist.*

> *I vowed that I was going to grow up and be... just like Mrs. Taylor* (*Newsweek*, special edition, Summer 1991).

1. Was there a "Mrs. Taylor" in your life, a woman whose example profoundly impacted you? If so, share briefly how she did.

Memorize the following:

> *Give her the reward she has earned, and let her works bring her praise at the city gate* (Prov. 31:31).

2. Read the following and explain how a godly woman's works endure. What impresses you?

   A. *The memory of the righteous will be a blessing* (Prov. 10:7a).

   B. *A kindhearted woman gains respect* (Prov. 11:16a).

For no one can lay any foundation other than the one that has been laid; that foundation is Jesus Christ. Now if anyone builds on the foundation with gold, silver, precious stones, wood, hay, straw—the work of each builder will become visible, for the Day will disclose it, because it will be revealed with fire, and the fire will test what sort of work each has done. If what has been built on the foundation survives, the builder will receive a reward. If the work is burned up, the builder will suffer loss; the builder will be saved, but only as through fire (1 Cor. 3:11–15 NRSV).

DAY 2

She Finds Favor with God

Though the rain falls on the righteous and the unrighteous (Matt. 5:45), still, Scripture shows us that God gives special blessings to those who are faithful, who walk in integrity.

3. In the following verses, find the blessings that a woman walking in righteousness may experience. If you have experienced this blessing, share something about a specific time when you did:

■ Proverbs 1:32–33

■ Proverbs 3:3–10

■ Proverbs 3:33

■ Proverbs 15:29

■ Proverbs 28:13–14

4. Is there a blessing in your life for which you are particularly thankful right now? If so, what is it?

5. The book of Proverbs also repeatedly makes the point that "the way of the unfaithful is hard" (Prov. 13:15b). What are some of the griefs that we may be spared if we do not harden our hearts (based on the above proverbs or your own observations)?

DAY 3

She Finds Favor with Man

Though it is true that "everyone who wants to live a godly life in Christ Jesus will be persecuted" (2 Tim. 3:12), it is also true that many people will respect you, be at peace with you, and even show you favor.

6. In the following verses, discover how, and perhaps from whom, you may find favor if you walk in integrity.

■ Proverbs 11:24–25 (Compare to Luke 6:38.)

■ Proverbs 16:7

■ Proverbs 31:28–29

7. How have you experienced blessings from others as you have lived for Jesus?

8. Proverbs repeatedly shows that the wicked are despised by their fellow man. "The memory . . . of the wicked will rot" (Prov. 10:7 NRSV). What are some of the reasons the wicked are despised by others (based on Proverbs or your own observation)?

DAY 4

Jezebel, Out of Favor with God and Man

Queen Jezebel was an idolater, a liar, and a murderer. Her death was horrendously brutal and her memory, as Proverbs says will be true of the wicked, is rotten. Her very name has become synonymous with evil.

9. What can you discover about Jezebel's wickedness from the following passages?

■ 1 Kings 16:29–33

■ 1 Kings 19:1–2

■ 1 Kings 21

Proverbs 13:15a says "the way of the unfaithful is hard." Using your imagination, how do you think Jezebel's life might have been difficult?

10. Take a look at Jezebel's death.

   A. What prophecy did Elijah give concerning Jezebel's death in 1 Kings 21:23?

   B. Describe how Jezebel prepared to die in 2 Kings 9:30. What does this tell you about her heart?

   C. Describe her death in 2 Kings 9:31–37.

A faithful woman's example endures, as a sweet fragrance, but the example of the wicked is a stench. Jezebel's daughter Athaliah walked in her steps and murdered those in her way, even her own grandchildren (2 Kings 11:1).

DAY 5

Mary, Who Found Favor with God

Mary was honored above all women. As she realized, her memory would be precious: "all generations will call me blessed" (Luke 1:48). Would it not behoove us to study and emulate her? Two of Mary's many valuable attributes worthy of emulation were her faith and her servant heart, as captured in the following poem by Lucy Shaw:

Too much to ask

it seemed too much to ask

of one small virgin

that she should stake shame

against the will of God.

all she had to hold to

were those soft, inward flutterings

and the remembered sting

of a brief junction—spirit

with flesh.

who would think it

more than a dream wish?

an implausible, laughable defense.

and it seems much

too much to ask me

to be part of the

different thing—

God's shocking, unorthodox,

unheard of Thing

to further heaven's hopes

and summon God's glory.

Reprinted from *Polishing the Petoskey Stone*, by Luci Shaw, © 1990.
Used by permission of Harold Shaw Publishers, Wheaton, IL 60189.

One characteristic of Mary was that she had a desire to praise God. Before you begin in your quiet time today, sing "For the Beauty of the Earth" (p. 116) and "Father, I Adore You" (p. 114).

Read Luke 1:26–38.

11. After reading the above passage, examine the following questions.

    A. How did Gabriel affirm Mary?

B. Considering the risk, why do you think Mary responded to Gabriel as she did in verse 38?

C. What risks is God asking you to take with your life? How are you responding?

Read Luke 1:39–49.
12. After reading the above passage, examine the following questions.

A. Read verses 36 and 39. How is Mary responding to this news about Elizabeth? Why do you think she responds in this way?

B. Share a time when God spoke to you through His Word or another person.

Read Luke 1:50–56.
13. Review verses 50, 52–53. Write down ways Mary saw those who were faithful experience favor from God.

14. Mary obviously was familiar with Scripture, committed it to heart, and pondered it. What do you learn about her from Luke 2:19?

As you ponder God's faithfulness to you in your heart, what are some of the incidents that stand out to you and what did you learn from them?

Action Assignment

Put a small box on your dining table with a notepad and pen. Whenever you are aware of God's faithfulness, record how and the date. Encourage family members to do likewise. At the end of the month, read and ponder them together.

15. As you reflect on Mary's life, what were some of the difficulties she faced? How do you see evidence of God's faithfulness and presence with her in those difficulties?

16. *The Living Bible* paraphrases Proverbs 14:14 as "The backslider gets bored with himself; the godly man's life is exciting." Using your imagination, in what ways do you think Mary's life was exciting? And in what ways is your life exciting?

17. In what ways was and is Mary still being blessed for her faithfulness? Contrast this with Jezebel.

18. What do you expect to remember from this study?

PRAYER TIME

Close by singing "Father, I Adore You" (p. 114) in a round. Then pray in twos or conversationally, beginning with praise for God's faithfulness to you.

NEXT WEEK

Ask a few women to bring some paraphrases (such as *The Living Bible* or *The Message*) and other translations for next week's final review exercise.

Prayers & Praises

_____

_____

_____

_____

_____

_____

_____

_____

_____

_____

_____

_____

_____

_____

Ten

Review

As Mary pondered the things from God in her heart, let us do likewise!

WARMUP

Go around, giving women the freedom to pass, and ask: Of the Biblical women you've studied in this guide, who made the strongest impression on you? Why?

SCRIPTURE STUDY

DAY I

Her Heart (Lessons 1 and 2)

Review the following memory verses: Proverbs 31:30 and 4:23.

1. What has God impressed on your heart from the above memory verses?

2. What are some reasons a wise woman fears God?

3. How does fearing and loving God affect her life choices? Give some examples.

4. What are some ways a wise woman keeps her heart?

5. What do you remember about the following women? What will you learn from each?

   A. Sapphira

   B. The Hebrew midwives

   C. Mary of Bethany

   D. Martha of Bethany

DAY 2

She Is Discreet (Lessons 3 and 4)

Review the following memory verses: Proverbs 31:26 and 11:22.

6. What has God impressed on your heart from the above memory verses?

7. Define discretion. Give a few examples.

8. Contrast a woman of discretion and a woman of indiscretion in regard to the use of her tongue.

9. What do you remember about the following women? What will you learn from each?

    A. Euodia and Syntyche

    B. Hannah

    C. The women of Zion in Isaiah 3

    D. The holy women in 1 Peter 3

DAY 3

She Is Prudent and She Honors Her Husband (Lessons 5 and 6)

Review the following memory verses: Proverbs 19:14 and 31:10-12.

10. What has God impressed on your heart from the above memory verses?

11. How is prudence similar to discretion? How is it different?

12. How did the following women exemplify prudence or the lack of it? What do you remember from each?

    A. Zeresh

    B. Abigail

13. How did the following women honor or dishonor their husbands? What can you learn from them?

    A. Elizabeth

    B. Rebekah

DAY 4

She Is Diligent and Trains Her Children (Lessons 7 and 8)

Review the following memory verses: Proverbs 31:27–29.

14. What is God impressing on your heart from the above passage?

15. What do you remember from the following women? What did each teach you?

   A. The idle widows of 1 Timothy 5

   B. The diligent widows of 1 Timothy 5

   C. Herodias

   D. Lois and Eunice

DAY 5

She Receives Favor from God and Man (Lesson 9)

Review the following memory verse: Proverbs 31:31.

16. What are some of the ways a woman living wholeheartedly for the Lord is blessed?

17. What did you learn from the lives of each of the following women?

A. Jezebel

B. Mary, the mother of Jesus

Final Review Exercise

In the discussion group, divide into circles of three or four women and do the following:

1. Have one women say a simple sentence prayer, asking God to open your eyes to what He wants to impress on your heart.

2. Have another woman read Proverbs 31:10–12, 26–31 in a different translation. Every woman should listen for a phrase that stands out to her.

3. Now have each woman share the phrase that stood out to her with no additional comments.

4. Have another woman read the same verses in a different translation, perhaps a paraphrase.

5. Now have each woman share, "I see" or "I hear."

6. Have another woman read the same verses in another translation.

7. Now have each woman share one way God is speaking to her from this passage.

8. Now hold hands, and have each woman pray for the woman on her right, asking God to help her obey what He has shown her from this passage. If she cannot pray aloud, she can squeeze the next woman's hand to show that she is praying silently.

Leader's Helps

Your Role:
A Facilitator for the Holy Spirit and an Encourager

A Facilitator for the Holy Spirit

People remember best what they articulate themselves, so your role is to encourage discussion and keep it on track. Here are some things you can do to help:

1. Ask questions and allow silences until someone speaks up. If the silence seems interminable, rephrase the question, but don't answer it yourself!

2. Direct the group members to look in the Scripture for their answers. Ask: "Where in this passage can you find help for answering this question?"

3. Place chairs in as small a circle as possible. Space inhibits sharing.

4. Deal with the monopolizer:

   A. Pray not only for her control, but that you can help find ways to make her feel valued—for excessive talking often springs from deep emotional needs.

   B. Wait for her to take a breath and gently say, "Thanks, could we hear from someone else?"

   C. Go around the room with a question, giving people freedom to pass.

   D. Set down some ground rules at the beginning of the session. You can tell the group that you would like to hear from each person at least three times. So after they've spoken three times, they should give the shyer members time to gather the courage to speak up. When the problem is serious, pass out three pennies to each member one time, telling them, "Each time you speak, you spend a penny. When they are gone, give the others a chance to spend theirs."

   E. So often in the Christian community we fail to speak the truth in love.

Either we are silent and let problems destroy, or if we do speak, it is not direct and loving. If this problem is not getting better, you have a responsibility to take the monopolizer aside and speak the truth in love. Here is what you might say: "You share easily, but some women are so shy. They may have some wonderful things to say, but they need silences to gather the courage to speak up. I need your help." You could ask her for her ideas on how to help. She may surprise you! Some ideas are:

• Star two or three questions and share only on those.

• After she shares, she could say, "What does someone else think?"

• She could watch the shy women's faces and, if they seem like they have a thought, ask them if they do!

• Count to 10 before she shares to see if someone else will first.

5. The Action Assignments and memory work will be used mightily in your group members' lives. If they aren't doing these exercises, call a few from the group and ask them to be good examples with you. Soon the others will follow!

An Encourager

Most women who drop out of a group do so not because the study is too challenging, but because they don't feel valued. As a leader, these are some of the things you can do to help each woman feel valued:

1. Greet each woman warmly when she walks in the door. This meeting should be the high point of her week!

2. Affirm answers when you can genuinely do so: "Good insight! Great! Thank you!" And always affirm nonverbally with your eyes, a smile, a nod.

3. If a woman gives a wrong or off-the-wall answer, be careful not to crush her. You can still affirm her by saying, "That's interesting—What does someone else think?" If you feel her response must be corrected, someone in the group will probably do it. If they don't, space your correction so it doesn't immediately follow her response and is not obviously directed at her.

4. If this is an interdenominational group, set this ground rule: No one is to speak unfavorably of another denomination.

5. Plan an evening, lunch, or breakfast just to get to know each other. Play games, have a time of blessing each other, or just visit.

6. Send notes to absentees and postcards to the faithful in appreciation.

7. Don't skimp on the prayer time. Women's emotional and spiritual needs are met during the prayer time, so allot one third of your time for that.

Leader's Helps for Chapter 1

She Loves and Fears God

Distribute the guides ahead of time and assign Chapter 1.

WARMUP

Bring name-tags and write the women's first names in large letters. You want the opening question about Charity to start the group off with a bang—so call on a few enthusiastic members.

SCRIPTURE STUDY

Helps for Specific Questions

Question #4E: She has ignored the marriage covenant she made before God. You could have the group turn to Ecclesiastes 5:4-6 and read it. Then ask again, why does a person break his or her word to God? The basic problem is a lack of fear of the Lord.

Question #4F: The land is a picture of heaven, and more insight can be gained by comparing these verses to Psalm 1. The wise man who fears the Lord is like the tree planted by water in Psalm 1—the Lord watches over him. The foolish man who doesn't fear God becomes wicked and is like the chaff of Psalm 1 that is blown away, does not stand in the judgment, and does not inherit the good land of heaven.

Question #7: Be ready to share vulnerably yourself. Encourage many to share. This is also an opportunity to ask if anyone has been delivered from the fear of hell—and how.

Question #12: Scripture teaches both that wives should submit to their husbands (Eph. 5:22) and also that each of us will give an account to God (2 Cor. 5:10). When the two are in conflict, the historical model seems to be to obey God (Peter, Abigail). You might ask the group to give some examples of black-and-white issues where a woman would have to gently tell her husband she cannot do something.

Question #14A: Worked ruthlessly; told midwives to murder babies, threw boy babies into the Nile.

Leader's Helps for Chapter 2

Her Heart Is Fully Devoted to Christ

SCRIPTURE STUDY

Helps for Specific Questions

Question #11: Jesus was helping Martha to see that her attitude of self-pity was wrong and also affirming Mary for her devotion. Martha's phrase "don't you care" indicates her attitude.

PRAYER TIME

You may want to demonstrate conversational prayer for the group with three or four who will be able to show the importance of short prayers and praying by subject.

Leader's Helps for Chapter 3
She Speaks with Wisdom

Remember to bring pennies for the Action Assignment. Even if you do not have a monopolizer, this is a helpful assignment for the shy people, to encourage them to spend their pennies.

OPTIONAL DISCUSSION QUESTIONS

Circle the following questions to skip in discussion if you have a group that has trouble finishing on time: #2, #8, #11.

SCRIPTURE STUDY

Helps for Specific Questions

Question #2: If we are speaking insults, that is our nature. If we are also speaking praises, it is a cover-up, for you don't get both salt and fresh water from the same stream.

Question #10: Pave the way for honest sharing by giving an example of trouble you caused by poor use of your tongue.

Leader's Helps for Chapter 4

She Is Discreet

OPTIONAL DISCUSSION QUESTIONS

Circle the following questions to skip in discussion if you have a group that has trouble finishing on time: #1, #7, #13.

SCRIPTURE STUDY

Helps for Specific Questions

Question #3: Peter says that husbands who are nonbelievers may be won without a word—however, this is not a prohibition against speaking of the Lord to an unsaved husband. (See 1 Peter 3:15–16.)

Question #6: Sarah called Abraham her lord. Today, a woman might show respect by taking his name in marriage, wearing a wedding ring, and never correcting him or speaking disparagingly of him in public. Your group can probably think of more!

PRAYER TIME

Demonstrate praying through Scripture with a friend before you send them off in pairs to do it.

Leader's Helps for Chapter 5
She Is Prudent

OPTIONAL DISCUSSION QUESTIONS

Circle the following questions to skip in discussion if you have a group that has trouble finishing on time: #4, #5.

SCRIPTURE STUDY

Helps for Specific Questions

Action Assignment

I have found it helpful to prioritize with A's (must do), B's (should do), and C's (could do). I pray and make my list. Here's an example:

A-1 Quiet time

A-2 Shower and dress

A-3 Pick up house

A-4 Finish rough draft of Chapter 3

A-5 Pick up new neighbor and take her to Bible study

B-1 Calls: Dentist, Carol, and Mother

B-2 Vacuum

B-3 Write sympathy note to Mrs. Erickson

C-1 Walk with Jean

After discussion, you may decide to extend this Action Assignment into next week.

Question #13B: Direct them to find ways in 1 Samuel 25:18, 23–26, 28.

Leader's Helps for Chapter 6

She Honors Her Husband

WARMUP

Tell them not to worry about repetition, for God often uses repetition to bring home a point.

OPTIONAL DISCUSSION QUESTIONS

Circle the following questions to skip in discussion if you have a group that has trouble finishing on time: #8, #9.

SCRIPTURE STUDY

Helps for Specific Questions

Question #9: We all sin (1 John 1:10). It is what we do with that sin that determines whether or not we have a clear conscience (1 John 1:9).

Question #10: Evidences that Elizabeth spent time with God and therefore knew His character can be found in Luke 1:6, 25, 42–45.

Leader's Helps for Chapter 7
She Finds Her Work to Be a Joy

OPTIONAL DISCUSSION QUESTIONS

Circle the following questions to skip in discussion if you have a group that has trouble finishing on time: #1, #4, #9.

SCRIPTURE STUDY

Helps for Specific Questions

Question #1: Ask: What kind of attitude inspires confidence?

Question #2: You may want to go around with this question, giving women the freedom to pass.

Question #15: Verse 13 talks about "going house to house." If time permits, you could ask when the use of the telephone becomes idleness.

Question #16: Spiritually dead.

Leader's Helps for Chapter 8

She Trains Her Children

If you have mothers with children at home, you may very well have difficulty finishing this in one lesson. I would suggest that instead of skipping questions, that you divide it into two weeks. Take the first two days the first week and the last three the second.

SCRIPTURE STUDY

Helps for Specific Questions

Question #13: "Like mother, like daughter" is taken from Ezekiel, and is actually used in a negative way. Surely that was true of Herodias and Salome!

Question #15: Often it seems easier to look the other way when your children disobey, but that's only short-term—it is far, far harder long-term.

Explaining the Gospel So That Even a Child Could Understand

Explain this during the study, using the following illustration.

1. Hold one hand up to represent God. God is holy (Isa. 6:3).

2. Drop the second hand far below the "holy hand" to represent the sinfulness of man. Man has fallen short of the holiness of God (Rom. 3:23).

3. God is just. He must punish sin (Rom. 3:25). Make a fist with the holy hand and hit the fallen hand.

4. But God is also merciful. Therefore He sent Jesus to die on a cross to take the punishment we deserve (Rom. 3:24). If we trust in Jesus, asking Him to be our Savior, God covers us with the righteousness of Christ. And though our sins may be as red as scarlet, now, when God looks down, they are as white as snow (Isa. 1:18). Show a white napkin covering the fallen hand.

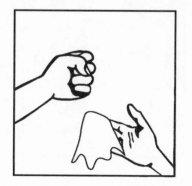

5. However, if we do not trust in God's provision, then we are not covered. (Remove napkin.) And God's wrath will hit us. Make a fist with the holy hand and hit the fallen hand (John 3:36).

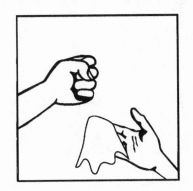

Leader's Helps for Chapter 9

She Finds Favor

OPTIONAL DISCUSSION QUESTIONS

Circle the following questions to skip in discussion if you have a group that has trouble finishing on time: #1, #2, #10. You want to be sure you pace yourself to get to Mary—summarize Jezebel if you must, but don't skimp on Mary. Her model will inspire and lead to good sharing.

SCRIPTURE STUDY

Helps for Specific Questions

Question #9: Have them describe some of the emotions they see in Jezebel and how those kinds of emotions affect you. Also, describe Jezebel's reputation. How would they feel if that was their reputation?

Question #12A: Help them to see that Mary hurried. You might have them look at a map to see the distance between Nazareth and the hill country of Judea (outside of Jerusalem). Hopefully they will see that it was important to her to make this long trip because she was being sensitive to the Spirit's leading.

Question #12B: While God seldom speaks to us through angels, He does still speak to us. You might call on people if they look like they might have something to share!

Question #14: If time permits, go around with this one!

Leader's Helps for Chapter 10

Review

OPTIONAL DISCUSSION QUESTIONS

When you have 20 minutes left, skip to the final review exercise.

FINAL REVIEW EXERCISE

This exercise, taken from "The African Model," is powerful. Remind the women to:

1. Pause and meditate before answering.

2. Use various Bibles, such as *The Living Bible* or *The Amplified Bible*.

3. Share only the phrase—no comment—in Step 3.

Memory Verses

Chapter 1
Charm is deceptive, and beauty is fleeting; but a woman who fears the LORD is to be praised (Prov. 31:30).

Chapter 2
Keep thy heart with all diligence; for out of it are the issues of life (Prov. 4:23, KJV).

Chapter 3
She speaks with wisdom, and faithful instruction is on her tongue (Prov. 31:26).

Chapter 4
Like a gold ring in a pig's snout is a beautiful woman who shows no discretion (Prov. 11:22).

Chapter 5
Houses and wealth are inherited from parents, but a prudent wife is from the LORD (Prov. 19:14).

Chapter 6
A wife of noble character who can find? She is worth far more than rubies. Her husband has full confidence in her and lacks nothing of value. She brings him good, not harm, all the days of her life (Prov. 31:10–12).

Chapter 7
She watches over the affairs of her household and does not eat the bread of idleness (Prov. 31:27).

Chapter 8
Her children arise and call her blessed; her husband also, and he praises her: "Many women do noble things, but you surpass them all" (Prov. 31:28–29).

Chapter 9
Give her the reward she has earned, and let her works bring her praise at the city gate (Prov. 31:31).

Music

Closing with a song helps people leave a small group meeting with their focus on Jesus. Music Minister John Haines makes the following suggestions for a successful song time.

1. Teach the song the first time. Be sure you know it. If you cannot do this, delegate it to someone who can. Even if it is a familiar chorus to many, teach it the first time—for there will be those who don't know it.

2. Sing the song in a relatively low key.

Doxology

For the Beauty of the Earth

Folliott S. Pierpoint, altered

Conrad Kocher; arr. William H. Monk

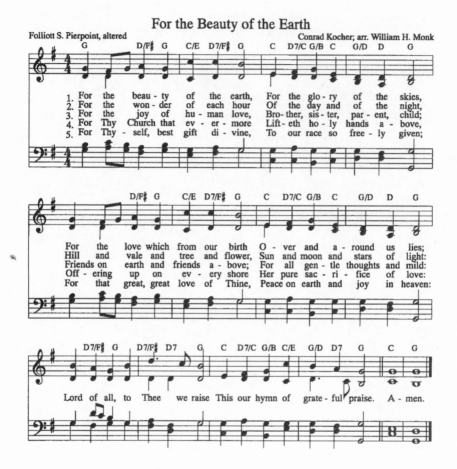

1. For the beau - ty of the earth, For the glo - ry of the skies,
2. For the won - der of each hour Of the day and of the night,
3. For the joy of hu - man love, Bro - ther, sis - ter, par - ent, child;
4. For Thy Church that ev - er - more Lift - eth ho - ly hands a - bove,
5. For Thy - self, best gift di - vine, To our race so free - ly given;

For the love which from our birth O - ver and a - round us lies;
Hill and vale and tree and flower, Sun and moon and stars of light:
Friends on earth and friends a - bove; For all gen - tle thoughts and mild:
Off - ering up on ev - ery shore Her pure sac - ri - fice of love:
For that great, great love of Thine, Peace on earth and joy in heaven:

Lord of all, to Thee we raise This our hymn of grate - ful praise. A - men.

Turn Your Eyes Upon Jesus

Words and Music by
Helen Lemmel

Cares Chorus

Kelly Willard